Fly Fishing
ROCKY MOUNTAIN NATIONAL PARK

Fly Fishing

ROCKY MOUNTAIN NATIONAL PARK

An Angler's Guide

TODD HOSMAN

PRUETT PUBLISHING COMPANY
BOULDER, COLORADO

Printed in the United States
10 9 8 7 6 5 4 3 2 1

Library of Congress Cataloging-in-Publication data

Hosman, Todd, 1957–
    Fly fishing Rocky Mountain National Park : an angler's guide /
Todd Hosman.
        p.   cm.
    Includes bibliographical references and index.
    ISBN 0-87108-876-2
    1. Fly fishing—Colorado—Rocky Mountain National Park—
Guidebooks. 2. Rocky Mountain National Park (Colo.)—Guidebooks.
I. Title.
SH475.H67   1996
799.1'755—dc20   96-5440
                                                              CIP

Contents

We were a noisy crew; the sun in heaven
Beheld not vales more beautiful than ours;
Nor saw a band in happiness and joy
Richer, or worthier of the ground they trod.
I could record with no reluctant voice
The woods of autumn, and their hazel bowers
With milk-white clusters hung; the rod and line,
True symbols of hope's foolishness, whose strong
And unreproved enchantment led us on
By rocks and pools shut out from every star,
All the green summer, to forlorn cascades
Among the windings hid of mountain brooks.

—William Wordsworth, *The Prelude: Book First*

1

Rocky Mountain National Park:
Fly Fishing at Its Best

L ocated in north-central Colorado less than a two-hour drive from Denver, Rocky Mountain National Park covers over 265,000 acres and spans the Continental Divide. Within the Park, hundreds of trails weave through a dramatically varied landscape of snowy mountain peaks, flower-filled glacial meadows, pine forests, aspen groves, and alpine tundra. Throughout this grandly beautiful place flow countless streams and several rivers. Lakes abound too, along with innumerable ponds and creeks. But of the Park's annual three million visitors, most come to sightsee, hike, or take photographs. Hardly anyone casts a line. So, many Park waters remain largely overlooked and seldom fished, even though they may be filled with healthy, hungry trout—brookies, cutthroats, rainbows and browns—none of them stocked, but all wild and self-sustaining.

What's the catch? Small fish. In fact, anglers preoccupied with hooking trophy-sized trout may not even want to make the trip here. Because of a short and difficult growing season, most trout caught in the Park measure only about eight inches long, and a ten-incher is a prize indeed. Regardless of size, every fish is a winner—gorgeous, crafty, and vibrant. And every fish lives in one of the world's most enchanting areas. For what it's worth, I'd rather spend an evening casting to little wild brookies in an unknown, uncrowded, and unspoiled Park creek than a day hauling in big stocked rainbows on some name-brand river with a parking lot next to it. This book is for fly anglers who might share that same perspective.

Park waters change with the seasons, remaining frozen over between November and March. Typically, rivers and streams become nearly free of ice by late March. During this period of ice-out, flows are low, slow, and cold (about 38 degrees Fahrenheit), but trout nonetheless begin feeding after their winter of relative inactivity. Runoff begins by April or May: mountain snowpack starts to melt and waters eventually rise to their highest levels by about mid-June. By early July runoff abates, and stream flows begin to moderate and become more predictable. By late August water temperatures have peaked at around 55 or 60 degrees, and waters run low and clear until refreezing (ice-in) occurs, usually in mid-November. The early and late seasons—a few weeks after ice-out and several weeks before ice-in—offer some of the best fishing, though few anglers are around to take advantage of it. The Park and the surrounding area then are unusually quiet, and the trout seem especially anxious to strike at a well-presented fly. In addition, trout often feed more aggressively during their spawning seasons. (Cutthroats and rainbows spawn in the spring, brookies and browns in the fall.) By and large, though, a dedicated fly angler can do well at nearly any time in the Park—just as long as there's some open water. Get ready for a long and wonderful season.

Though Park fishing does not require a special permit, just a Colorado fishing license, some special regulations are enforced, a few of which are listed here. Everyone over the age of thirteen who fishes must use only artificial flies or lures equipped with a single hook. Children twelve and under may use bait. Regardless of the angler's age, some waters are restricted solely to barbless catch-and-release fishing with artificial flies or lures, and others are closed to fishing altogether. The size and number limits on any fish to be kept vary; check with the Park Information Center. To help perpetuate the natural growth of this wild, self-sustaining fishery—a very rare and cherished thing these days—most dedicated fly anglers practice catch-and-release fishing.

Certainly the dominant fish in the Park is the trout; other fish (like suckers and minnows) are comparatively few. In identifying trout, remember that water conditions, time of year, location, diet, and gender can all profoundly affect a fish's appearance. And all four major Park trout species may inhabit the same water. For these reasons, even if you refer to color photographs, it can be difficult or practically impossible to distinguish a brook from a brown, or a rainbow from a cutt. The following comments and descriptions are general guidelines for recognizing and locating Park trout.

Of all trout species in the Park, brook trout (brookies) are the most numerous. They are remarkably adaptable to varying water conditions and temperatures. In fast, slow, still, or rushing water, near or far from shore, you'll catch brookies. They can be identified by their bright orange fins that are tipped in snow white and jet black. Their bodies are often spotted with blue.

Rainbow trout have silvery, iridescent bodies with a dark, somewhat diffuse charcoal-and-pink horizontal bar along the side, and red around the gills. The spotted body of a greenback cutthroat may vary in color from light to very dark green. Probably the most pronounced feature is its "cut throat"—the gill areas and underside of the mouth can be brilliant scarlet. It's especially easy to confuse a rainbow with a cutt. Prime holding areas for rainbows and cutts include pools, shady spots, deeper pockets of water near shore, and the sides of large rocks. Compared to brookies, rainbows and cutts prefer areas of cooler temperatures in still or moving waters.

The greenback cutthroat trout was fished commercially almost to extinction in the early 1900s. Today the Park Service periodically "plants" wild greenbacks from other areas into appropriate Park waters in usually successful efforts to restore the species to its original habitats. *The greenback is a threatened species and any specimens caught must be immediately returned unharmed to the water.* A few Park waters hold Colorado River cutts. The similarity between these fish and greenbacks is striking. To confuse matters further, there are hybrids of rainbows and various cutts, called "cuttbows," that also can strongly resemble greenbacks. I'd advise that if you catch anything that makes you even think about a greenback cutt, you'd better set that fish free in a hurry.

The brown trout has a light bronze body marked by black spots and red spots encircled by blue. Its fins are primarily light bronze;

they are not colorfully tipped, as are the brookie's. Browns are the most shy and wary of all trout species in the Park. One of their preferred holding areas is undercut banks. Fish for browns in the early morning, at dusk, or on days of low light, when they often venture into still waters to feed. Like brook trout, browns tolerate a wide range of water temperatures and conditions. But although you may see brookies, rainbows, and cutts at altitudes from 7,000 to 11,000 feet, you'll seldom catch a brown at an elevation above 9,000 feet.

Trip Preparation

Before you head out with suitcase and rod in hand, realize that the Park is not as idyllic as it may first appear. Sadly, like so many other national parks, Rocky Mountain has developed a reputation as something of a playground, petting zoo, or theme park. And in the interest of perpetuating a tourist industry and avoiding bad press, nearby communities tend to downplay or avoid mention of Park problems. Not uncommonly, however, people do get seriously injured and killed here—most often unnecessarily. At some trailheads you'll see signs posted by the Park Service: "The mountains don't care." In other words, as much as we might love the Park's wildness, we had damn well better respect it. For your comfort, enjoyment, and safety, you'll need to become familiar with some characteristics and peculiarities of the Park area before venturing on that first trip.

On Park Roads

The first time you arrive in the Park, you'll probably be driving. And probably the single most dangerous creature you'll ever encounter in the Park is a person operating a motor vehicle thoughtlessly. Many motorists here become so overcome and distracted by scenery that they pay little attention to anything else, and accidents inevitably ensue. If, while driving, you are dumbstruck by the sight of a sunset, mountain range or moose, don't swerve, slam on your brakes, and stop in the middle of the road to get a better look. Such a sequence of events sounds crazy, but it happens all the time in the Park. Of course, you should instead use your turn signals, pull off onto a parking area, turn off your engine, and then enjoy the view.

As you drive the area's steep roads, pay attention to how much you use your brakes because burned-out brakes are a common occurrence here. Brake only when you really have to—downshift instead, or just take your foot off the accelerator. Since most visitors are not accustomed to mountain roads, they tend to travel too fast or too slowly, in either case posing a hazard to other drivers. Posted speed limits are realistic and safe guidelines, but if the pace feels uncomfortably quick, pull off at the first open shoulder, let others pass you, and then proceed. Traveling in excess of the speed limit is out of the question. Area roads were not designed for fast driving and, furthermore, large animals like deer and elk often appear seemingly out of nowhere—right in front of you. Locally, it's customary to flash your headlights to warn other vehicles of animals you've seen on or near the road.

Wildlife: What To Expect

One of the reasons you'll see deer close to the road is because that's where misguided people have been feeding them. Throughout Colorado, feeding wild animals is illegal and dangerous. The act threatens their health and well-being by tainting their natural diets, reducing their independence, and encouraging them to congregate in areas where they'll just end up as roadkill. Wild creatures can also bite, kick, claw, or trample you, and they carry transmittable diseases such as rabies. Over time, animals fed by humans can become so fearless of people that they become a perilous nuisance and must be destroyed.

Keep your distance from all wild animals. Even the most benign-looking deer, for example, may become justly annoyed by your approach and charge in retaliation. While in Park waters, however, especially those in meadows, you may find yourself suddenly in the midst of an elk herd that silently gathered as you were concentrating on fishing. That's happened to me dozens of times. I've found that if I just continue to behave naturally, the elk show no particular interest in me, though some seem fascinated by the sight of a cast line or the sound of a clicking reel. When I'm ready to leave the area, though, I move in a direction that's clearly away from (and so unthreatening to) the herd.

By chance, I have been in uncomfortably close quarters with elk. In one instance, I was standing in the middle of a stream when I noticed a pretty spotted elk calf standing on the bank to my right. The pleasure I took in the sight lasted only a moment before I realized that the calf's mother had to be nearby. And so she was—on the stream's opposite bank. That made me the only real obstacle between her and the crying baby. The big cow was clearly displeased, slowly and repeatedly tilting her head toward me and showing the whites of her eyes. I stayed in the water and began slowly moving away, making no effort to maintain eye contact with the cow but occasionally glancing in her direction just to see what she was doing. (She was waiting for me to leave.) And as I waded, I spoke in a soft, even, and reassuring tone, a technique once suggested to me by a large-animal veterinarian. I'm sure my monologue was far from brilliant, but at least I got out of there without any hoofprints on me.

Keep in mind that I've made thousands of fly-fishing trips into the Park and that any close calls I've had with wildlife have been few. However, two other large mammals, the black bear and the puma (or mountain lion) merit comment. Both animals are relatively uncommon in the Park, but it's prudent to know what to do if you see them. If, from a distance, you see one or the other, walk—don't run or jog—in the opposite direction. Though there have been sightings of pumas in the Park, there have been no recently recorded attacks of pumas upon humans in the area. In all of Colorado for the past several years, pumas have killed a few people who were running or jogging, usually in the early morning or around twilight. Naturalists theorize that the big cats prefer a moderately fast-moving prey because it's easier to kill. Pumas are inherently shy creatures, and I've never heard of any angler meeting one face-to-face in the Park.

Bears also are shy and infrequently seen. Perhaps because of high visitor use or marginally appropriate habitat in the Park, its bears forage at night and bed down during the day—reversing "normal" bear behavior. On the remote chance that you encounter a bear up close, act calmly and back off slowly without showing any signs of aggression or fear.

Demands of Climate and Terrain

Depending on where you stay and what your destinations are, you'll likely be spending time at elevations ranging between about 7,500 feet and 12,000 feet above sea level. No matter how healthy and well conditioned they may be, many visitors experience altitude sickness. The more common symptoms include headache, dizziness, nausea, shortness of breath, and fatigue. Although altitude sickness generally passes after a few days' acclimation to the mountain environment, it can be a grave affliction. Don't hesitate to consult with a physician if you feel ill.

Since most of your outdoor activities in the Park will be in an atmosphere of reduced oxygen, increased dryness, and intensified sun, you should take some commonsense steps to protect yourself. Foremost is never to push yourself beyond your limits. If you feel tired out, stop where you are and rest. When you're nearly exhausted, overheated, or chilled, it's never worthwhile to try for one more mile on the trail or one more hour on the water—take a break, get comfortable, or just pack it in for the day. Since high-altitude sunlight is exceptionally powerful (even on overcast days), always use sunscreen. In addition, your body will be dehydrating quite rapidly, so be sure to take along and drink plenty of water—even if you don't feel thirsty. Never drink from rivers, streams, lakes, or ponds in the Park. As clean as the water appears, much of it contains *Giardia*, a microorganism from the excrement of beavers and other animals that causes serious illness in humans.

You should know that in the course of an otherwise unremarkable summer day in the Park, temperature swings of forty or fifty degrees are common, and mountain weather in general is highly unpredictable. Winds may suddenly gust over eighty miles an hour, and intense storms can appear without warning. Prepare yourself by dressing intelligently. Wear layers of clothing that can be removed or added to according to your needs and the demands of the environment. Hypothermia (a potentially deadly loss of body heat) can occur even when weather conditions seem relatively pleasant. So, feeling "just a little cool" for several hours can prove devastating. And regardless of how warm the air may be, if you somehow get soaked, change into dry clothing immediately. Otherwise, you may become hypothermic. If you feel continually chilled or otherwise uncomfortable, get yourself out of the Park and to some medical treatment.

A bit more on the subject of clothing—it's always a good idea to carry a lightweight rain jacket and an extra pair of socks. The best clothing colors are subdued grays, blues, and browns: they allow you to blend in more with the natural environment. A hat and polarized sunglasses are absolute necessities. Polarized lenses (preferably brown) cut through glare and enhance your ability to see into the water. They also protect your eyes from hooks, airborne debris, and branches. A baseball-style cap provides additional protection from the sun, improves your water vision, and helps shield your scalp and head from hooks.

From what I've observed, the most common mistake made by Park hikers is underestimating travel time and effort. On many evenings I've met backpackers at trailheads ready to set out on a six-mile hike to a camping area and get there before nightfall. When I ask how long they think their trip will take, the answer is usually something like, "About an hour and a half or two." I know some fine mountain horses who couldn't make such good time. Your rate of travel while hiking on Park trails will be only about one or two miles an hour, sometimes a little faster, often much slower, depending on the trail's condition and steepness, and how often and long you decide to rest en route.

You won't need any special mountaineering boots to hike Park trails, just a pair of good-quality sneakers. Still, many trails are of loose, crumbling rock that makes secure footing difficult. As long as you proceed slowly and carefully, you shouldn't have any problem. Two quick reminders: First, high mountain vegetation is delicate and can take hundreds of years to regrow, so stay on the trails. Second, you should be extraordinarily careful with fire in the Park throughout the year, but most especially in the summer and fall, when Park forests get tinder-dry. Check with the Park Service regarding fire-use regulations.

One hazard you're almost sure to encounter in your Park travels is lightning, which has killed quite a few people here. At the first hint of a thunderstorm, lower your fly rod and carry it low to the ground (or leave it behind entirely). Seek shelter at once, and stay there until the storm passes. Be forewarned: these storms can get quite strong (and loud). In general, they may last from a few minutes to a couple of hours. If you are in a stream or on a lake, get out of the water and into low-lying brushy areas away from solitary tall trees and other lightning attractors. If you are in a wide-open exposed area from which there is no immediate escape (such as a boulderfield or an expanse of tundra), crouch low to the ground with hands on knees. Keeping your head covered is a good idea too, because large hail often accompanies lightning-producing storms.

Your hike might require that you ford water, but realize that even the smallest Park stream can be treacherous during the runoff of spring and early summer. Water less than knee-deep can topple and overpower a strong man, so use your best judgment before deciding whether or not you can safely wade or cross. A stout wading staff that also doubles as a hiking stick (a few firms manufacture collapsible versions) may save you from an unwanted dip in icy waters. If you do fall into a stream or river, protect your head from the rocks! If you can't escape the currents, point your feet—not your head—downstream. You may be able to push off of rocks and other submerged obstacles until you reach shore. Steer clear of tangled deadfalls (old trees and roots) in the water; they can trap and drown you.

Fly Fishing Etiquette

Now that you've been presented with a series of facts about how easily we can all get freeze-dried, parboiled, and fricasseed by Mother Nature, let's take a quick look at a potentially less risky subject. Feeding fly anglers is okay, but they merit at least as much space as a bear. To avoid unpleasant situations, stay at least a couple hundred yards away from and out of sight of someone who's fishing. Even better, go someplace else—there's plenty of water. If you meet other anglers on the water, take the initiative: ask which way they're headed (so you can stay out of the way), maybe discuss fishing and trade some flies, and move on (unless you're invited to stay). You'll make a lot friends. If someone intrudes into your area, you have a couple of options. You can cordially inform them of the Rocky Mountain angling traditions that respect privacy and first-come, first-fished water rights, and politely suggest another place for them to go. This seldom works. A much better ploy is to ask them smilingly where they were planning to go after this, since after all, you want to stay out of *their* way. Then depart. They usually get the message.

2

Reading the Water,
Knowing the Fish

Biologists describe trout as opportunistic feeders: to conserve energy, trout eat the food that comes to them most easily. Consequently, a trout may ignore a fly the first time you present it but will take the fly on a presentation that drifts just a fraction of an inch closer. Besides food, trout seek good cover and oxygenated water, both of which abound in the Park. For a trout, there are two components of good cover: (1) protection from predators (and therefore, access to a route of escape) and (2) protection from the force of currents. Trout wait in the best holding areas (known as "lies") available to them to take advantage of food delivered by the currents. Usually, the fish position themselves facing upstream, into food-bearing flows. Socially, trout are hierarchical. The biggest and strongest take and defend the best feeding spots (or prime lies). Smaller and weaker trout are relegated to less desirable positions.

The Big Picture

In a body of water, variations in flows, textures, depths, and so on all affect the quality of trout lies. So, when you arrive at a stream, view its general character first. There are straight sections and ones that bend; surfaces that are smooth or rippled; stretches that are fast or slow, deep or shallow. Every transitional area ("seam") between waters of contrasting character represents a trout lie. Any object in or above the stream that affects water flow or environment is an obstacle. Obstacles also mark trout lies: for example, a partly or fully

11

submerged boulder, gravel bar, or other pronounced alteration of the streambed; a beaver dam, an overhanging tree, or the shoreline itself. That's how to make sense of a big picture: identify character, seams, and obstacles.

Four Major Water Types

While you could successfully fly fish in the Park by concentrating your efforts nearby, in, or around seams and obstacles, there are also four major water types that warrant attention: riffle, pool, run, and pocket water. Each in its own way (through current, depth, or both) can provide trout with necessary food, cover, and oxygen. Each water type contains its own sets of seams and obstacles. A riffle is shallow (sometimes only a few inches deep), quick water. A rocky bottom contributes to its agitated currents and broken surface. Basin-shaped and deep, a pool's currents may vary from calm to moderate. A run can be described as moderate- to fast-paced deep water that flows within fairly regular boundaries and has a noticeably dominant current. In pocket water, fast waters flow in conflicting currents, creating roughly pocket-shaped concavities that can measure from a few inches to several feet across.

A couple of the more prominent transitional areas shown in figure 1 include the head and tail of the pool (usually very good lies) and the seams between pocket water and run, and riffle and tail. Currents are seldom simple, and the pool contains two outstanding features you should look for in any water: an eddy and a backwater. An eddy is formed by swirling currents; it serves as a kind of feeding tube that drains down to the trout. In a backwater, a section of prevailing current turns back on itself, bringing along a high concentration of food.

All water types are interdependent. The most pretty pool in the Park, if fed by a dead riffle and drained into a lackluster run, probably won't fish well. On the other hand, that pool may be so spacious and full of food that the riffle above and the run below hold hardly any trout. The fact is, there are endless types of water that can provide excellent fishing. The question gets to be: How can you judge a water type's potential when a fishing book has no corresponding

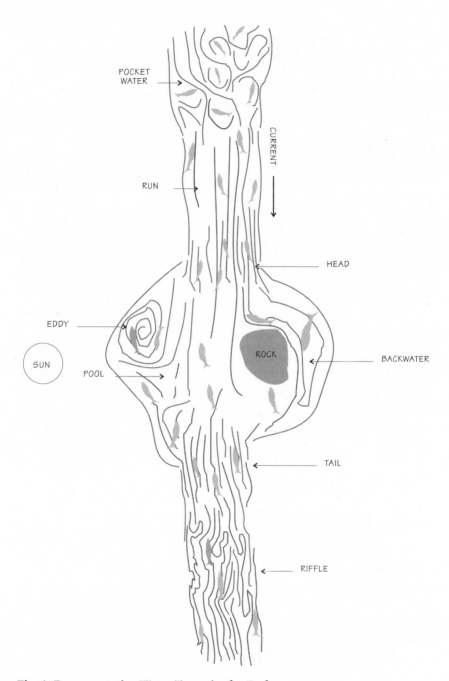

Fig. 1. Representative Water Types in the Park

diagram? Study the water in context of character, seams, and obstacles. After determining the water type on the larger scale, continue to apply your analysis on progressively smaller bases until you have a target area measured in feet or, better yet, inches. Do you think food, cover, and oxygen are sufficient? Then get ready to fish.

Before You Begin To Cast

One of the worst mistakes a fly angler can make is to head straight for the single best-looking spot, carelessly wading through or otherwise putting down (frightening into a cessation of feeding) the trout both en route to and in the target area. It's a chain reaction. Your walking through the riffle (or fishing it poorly) spooks the trout in the tailwater, and some of them dash madly into the pool, frightening the residents there, and so on. Therefore, when you arrive at any fishing destination, always take the time—at *least* five or ten minutes, and often much longer—to observe the surroundings. Then ask yourself some questions:

- Are there bugs in the air, in the water, under streambed rocks, or on the leaves or shore? If so, what kind, and how are they behaving?
- What is the direction of sunlight and wind?
- What are the water and weather conditions?
- Can you see what are the trout up to, and where?
- Can you hear them? (It happens.)
- Can you smell them? Large numbers of voraciously feeding trout emit a faint scent of watermelon. (Some of you think this a bad joke; others know I'm not kidding. Those who have gone after bluefish will at least acknowledge the possibility.)

Another extremely important question in the Park is: What are other animals doing?

- The ouzel (or dipper) is a small slate-colored, short-bodied waterbird that enjoys eating much the same food that trout do—usually a sign the fish are nearby.

- A herd of elk or deer crossing a stream kicks up quite a bit of insect life, causing trout downstream to begin feeding actively.
- In their labors, beavers and muskrats release nymphs and larvae into the flows.
- Are swallows or other small birds swooping through the air? They're likely after midges, mayflies, or some other aquatic insect also of interest to trout.
- Is a kingfisher (a crested, long-billed, blue-and-white predatory bird that feeds on small fish) in sight? How about a great blue heron, stalking the same prey? Little fish usually indicate the presence of larger ones.

You're fly fishing in an area that's not only beautiful but volatile and complex. Your questions and their answers can vary from one day—or one minute—to the next.

Seeing the Fish

Trout are easiest to spot when you're looking down from an elevation, for example a streambank, bridge, or rock. (As mentioned previously, polarized lenses and a cap are necessities. And don't give your presence away to the fish. Some elements of stealth are described in Chapter 4.)

There are two good ways to spot trout. The first is to focus your vision on a single section of likely water measuring no more than about two feet across. Once your eyes become accustomed to the view, continue to look there for at least a minute or two, then move on to another water section. The second method is to find a relatively smooth portion of the water's surface (smooth clear spots exist even in riffles and pockets). That glassy portion of water becomes a moving window. Follow its course with your eyes and look for what's below the surface. Especially in moving water, the trout will appear as dark shadows, often moving subtly side to side or darting away so quickly as to make you wonder what, if anything, you just saw. A lot of fine anglers won't even begin to fish until they've spotted some trout. If you already know where the fish are, you're way ahead in the game.

Approaching the Water and the Trout

Looking back at figure 1, imagine it's ten o'clock in the morning on an October day with clear skies and bright sun. There's an occasional light upstream breeze and moderately low water. The pool is about forty feet across, the tail-riffle and head-run-pocket-water sections are each about twelve feet wide and twenty-five feet long. It seems that upstream presentations will work best. From where do you approach? The sun is on the stream's left, so plan on placing yourself between the sun and the fish. (The trout will see just sunlight, not you.)

Should you wade or stay on shore? Though many Park streams have fairly thick brushy shorelines, you may be able to make some presentations from dry land. When you must wade, move slowly and quietly. Approach each area in a way that's least likely to disturb the fish. After landing and reviving a trout, try to release the fish downstream so it doesn't spook your target areas upstream. This is the order in which I'd fish the water shown in figure 1.

1. Riffle
2. Tail
3. Pool, lower left
4. Pool, lower center
5. Eddy
6. Pool, center
7. Head
8. Run
9. Pocket water

You've probably noticed that no mention was made of fishing the right side of the pool, in particular, the great looking backwater and the rock to its left. For now, given the sun, calm weather, and other factors, I'd skip that area and return under more favorable low-light conditions of dusk. I'd fish from the right bank then, using short-line, high-rod presentations, and I'd probably target the backwater first, where I'd hope to get the best fish. If I did, I'd probably sacrifice the chance to catch trout on the upstream and downstream sides of the rock, but I wouldn't care! And if I didn't catch the back-water fish, I'd move my attention to the two trout by the rock, be-ginning with the downstream one. If caught, it would likely run down into the riffle and so still give me a chance at its upstream neighbor.

High Water Problems and Opportunities

Several years ago during runoff, I stood fifty feet from the Big Thompson River in the Park. Had someone been at my side, the wa-ter's roar would have made it necessary to yell to be heard. But above that noise came an even louder one, low-pitched and uniden-tifiable. Looking in its direction, I saw the shoreline shake. An instant later, a twenty-foot section of the bank, complete with full-grown trees, ripped free and bobbed downstream like a runaway island. Stream-flow records of 1991 show the Big Thompson in the Park peaking at about 1,000 cubic feet per second (cfs) on June 2, a huge increase over the already impressive 600 cfs of the previous day. By comparison, during April through mid-May, flows measured between 25 to 125 cfs and then climbed steadily to their June peaks. Water re-turned to bearable wading conditions (about 200 to 250 cfs) by mid-July and continued to improve as the summer progressed. (In contrast, the Big Thompson in the U.S. Route 34 canyon, below the dam, is a tailwater with flows seldom allowed to exceed 125 cfs.) The onset of warmer temperatures, more and stronger sunlight, and rains all encourage the snowmelt that comprises most runoff water. Especially in relatively low-lying fishing areas, the runoff season is also ideal for flash floods, which can occur in seconds with little warning. One thing to watch for is an inexplicable slowing down or lowering of the water where you are. It may indicate a jam of logs or debris upstream that's waiting to break loose. So look out! Make sure, when you fish in these conditions, that you are always aware of and able to reach escape routes to higher ground.

Too many fly anglers are creatures of habit. If they caught a good trout twenty years ago with a #10 Royal Wulff in a particular pool, they keep going back to the same water with the same fly, year after year, though the fishing is poor. A similarly narrow view is brought to the sight of high water. The river is a torrent, the angler reasons. It doesn't look right and it can't be fished. Nevertheless, one overlooked high-water opportunity is the shoreline, and up tight against it is one of the best areas to fish. There, trout don't have to work as hard to maintain position against the currents, which funnel to them a fine selection of both aquatic and terrestrial bugs. (A black #12 or #14 Woolly Worm can work wonders.)

Maybe the most neglected area is where dry land used to be before the banks overflowed. The rivulets and pools formed there may appear improbably small and inconsequential, but they can still hold trout. You might fish yards away from the site of the original riverbanks and catch trout in tiny new creeks barely two feet across and six inches deep—and often with dry flies, too. Mostly, though, you'll find that nymphs and other subsurface flies work best. During runoff, try heavily weighted brown or olive caddis larva patterns in sizes #10 and #12.

If you've ever had the experience of diving under ocean waves, you will recall that the water beneath is relatively calm, and so it is in a trout stream. Fast high water won't prevent you from catching trout as long as you can get your fly to or near the bottom. Prepare to use lots of weight and to lose some flies. A sinking-tip line (with a sink rate of about four inches per second) can be a big advantage, so bring a spare spool or reel that holds some.

Only about thirty years ago streamers were thought a sporting and prominent part of fly fishing. Times, tastes, and fashions changed, and use of the streamer in trout fishing was largely relegated to high and discolored water. Though streamers are mentioned here in that context, it's not their exclusive domain. In Park rivers, lakes, and streams at high and low elevations you can successfully use streamers in nearly all water conditions. Fish them with or without weight, on floating or sinking-tip lines. Casting down and across the current is one of the easiest ways to present a streamer. Once the streamer hits the water, the current pulls the line into a bow shape. The submerged streamer "swings" and then rises into its position at the end of an extended and straight line (see figure 2). It's a little like making a bank shot in pool.

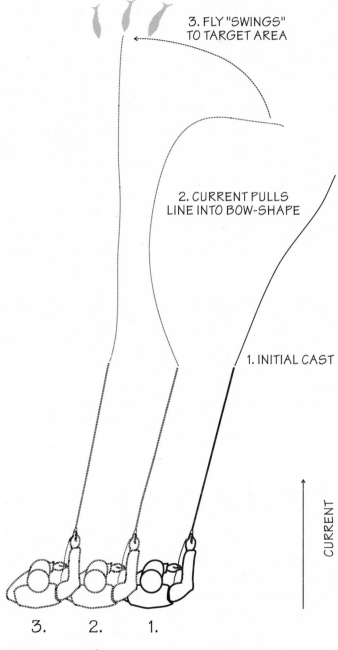

Fig. 2. Down-and-Across Streamer Presentation

After the streamer has reached its extended position, fish it by slowly moving the rod tip up and down or side to side, taking in or letting out a few inches of line (very slowly or very fast) and generally trying to make the streamer look like a good meal to the trout. During the retrieve, hold the rod off to one side of your body. Keep the rod tip low to the water and maintain a 90-degree angle between rod tip and line. Retrieve the streamer by stripping the line, twitching the rod tip, or both. Streamer retrieves work best when they are either extremely slow (about two inches or less per second) or rapid—as fast as you can strip back the line. Moderately paced retrieves are seldom productive. A trout usually takes a streamer vigorously, but be prepared for a take at nearly any time during a presentation. Pay as much attention to a streamer in the water as you would to a drifting dry fly or nymph. The best Park streamers are the Gray Ghost, Little Brook Trout, Woolly Bugger, Woolly Worm and Spruce Fly, all in sizes #8 to #14.

Contending with Wind

In the Park, both winds and streams tend to move in the same direction, which makes fly casting more challenging. If you'd like a lot of water to yourself, plan on fishing in a near-gale. Besides conferring the benefit of solitude, choppy waters also make trout less spooky and more indiscreet. Whether you cast upstream or down, the wind will take a toll, if you let it, on your back cast, forward cast, or both. Many anglers approach casting in the wind (considered here as a sustained blow of over fifteen miles per hour) with the wrong premise: They think only a short line is controllable then. In fact, only a longer line serves well, as its weight taps into the rod's power. And if ten feet of your thirty-foot cast blows back at you, fine—you've still cast twenty feet. Just be sure to get quick control of the slack line. A near-vertical rod position can be counterproductive because the rod shaft and line are wind-resistant. Instead, try casting with the rod kept low and horizontal to the water. Whatever rod position you use, concentrate on a compact and powerful casting stroke to produce the smallest possible line loops. They'll cut through wind most efficiently.

In windy conditions, fast line speeds work better than slow ones. If you can double-haul, do it. If you can't, learn. Here's a brief description: At the moment the back cast forms its loop, use your line hand (positioned a few inches above the grip and very close to the rod) to rapidly pull about a foot of line down toward your feet. That's a single haul, and its action will increase the speed of the line as it moves out in back of you. Learn to single-haul first. The action of the second haul is the same but performed as part of the forward cast. It may feel more awkward than the initial single haul did and should be practiced separately. When you can combine hauling on both the forward cast and the back cast, you've learned to double-haul.

Besides small loops, high line speed, a lowered rod, and extra line length, use at least a 5- or 6-weight rod. Overloading a rod by one or two line weights (for example, placing a 5- or 6-weight line on a 4-weight rod) can help, too. These are the simplest solutions to the problems of wind-casting, with one exception: You can always look for (and usually find) a sheltered spot where the wind isn't blowing as hard.

Fishing Park Lakes

Although Park lakes and ponds can offer excellent angling opportunities, some waters are barren. See Chapter 7 for a list of the best lake-fishing destinations, and always check with the Park Service for the most recent regulations. Just when lake ice-out occurs depends on the winter's severity, the spring's warmth, and the lake's altitude. On average, lakes will be free of ice by mid-June and ice will return by mid-October.

As a four-year-old, I learned to fly fish on a lake. I'd cast a wet fly out as far as I could (maybe ten feet), wait a while, and then strip it back either very slowly or very fast. The technique worked then and it works today, and that's the condensed version of how to fly fish Park lakes. A few years later, I was introduced to fly fishing on rivers and streams. I thought of the moving waters as more similar to lakes than different from them, and it's still a good perspective. Once you've arrived at a lake, identify character, seams, and obstacles. A lake's dominating obstacle is its shoreline, and that's where you'll find most plant and animal life, including trout. Take advantage of high clear banks to locate trout visually. You'll often see trout sunning themselves and feeding in shallow water just inches from dry land, so make plenty of your presentations parallel, not perpendicular, to the shoreline. While short casts will still catch trout, casts of up to fifty feet will prove useful. Other obstacles that warrant attention are like those in streams and rivers: rocks, stumps, overhanging trees, and so on. You'll find lots of them within casting distance of shore.

Fish in and around water seams (for example, areas between smooth and rippled water). They signify current formed by the wind, water flows, or both and are attractive lies because they tend to contain high concentrations of food. The transitional areas in and around inlet and outlet creeks are also excellent lies, as are places of significant change in water depth—a sandbar or drop-off, for example. The leeward shores (shores toward which the wind blows) will have some of the highest concentrations of food, and the trout will surely follow. Similarly, coves and other areas sheltered from wind and current are likely holding areas for trout food and trout. Although you'll want to use the lightest line possible (ideally a 3 or 4), the wind usually forces a trade-off to a heavier one, but don't exceed a 6-weight. Ten- to twelve-foot leaders are recommended.

If you decide to wade, hold your position in the water for at least ten minutes before beginning to cast. Not only will this give you the opportunity to reobserve your surroundings, but the trout will become accustomed to your presence, even feeding and swimming within arm's length. As you wade, move from one position to the next very slowly. You'll avoid spooking fish and will keep yourself from stepping into a deep hole or getting sucked into a murky bottom. Being stuck in two feet of mud is disconcerting at best. If you lose your balance, you won't merely fall in, you'll stay down for a while. If you do get bogged down in mud, keep one foot as solidly planted as you can while you slowly turn the other one from side to side and gradually raise it. With one foot free, work the other one the same way. Whatever you do, don't rush. The support and balance of a wading staff can be a big help in these situations.

Chapter 3 lists the best flies to use throughout the Park. The following comments apply especially to lakes. Dry flies should be sparsely tied, parachute, or both: caddis #12 to #20; mayfly #16 to #20; midge #18 to #24. Soft-Hackle flies (#10 to #18) make effective all-purpose emergers. Carry midge emergers in sizes #18 to #22. Bring a selection of nymphs and streamers, and don't forget the ants, sizes #14 to #22. Since swarms appear at high elevations, ants provide some of the best sport when fishing mountain lakes. Fish them as you would any dry fly, emerger, or nymph. After a cast, let the fly drift and wait a while, at least a few minutes. As always, follow the drift and control the line. If that fails, give slight intermittent twitches (about a half-inch every five to ten seconds) to the rod tip as the fly drifts. When they're not being drifted, nymphs, emergers, and streamers are most likely to catch a trout during a retrieve, which should be performed at an extreme: either very quickly or very slowly. During a slow retrieve, occasionally raising the rod tip, then pausing often precipitates a take.

Beaver Ponds

With only a few differences, the same techniques that yield results in lakes will prove worthwhile in beaver ponds. Ponds are best fished from the cover of low light (at dawn, dusk, or in overcast), in rain or snow, or when winds ruffle the water. Clear, bright, calm conditions seldom warrant your effort. Since most days in the Park are sunny and most ponds are sheltered from breezes by surrounding aspen and alder, you should generally fish toward evening, when bug activity on and in the pond is most intense. Show up an hour or two early just to observe. Add dams and lodges to your list of prime fishing areas. Browns and brookies in particular can be caught in very shallow water (less than four inches deep) adjoining a lodge. Even in a small pond, the water near a dam may exceed four feet in depth and hold fairly large trout. Ponds tend to be extremely silty, especially those near older, well-established dams, so wading should be kept to a minimum or avoided.

These are among the best flies for beaver ponds: Blue-Winged

Olive mayflies and Pheasant Tails, #16 to #20; parachute caddis patterns and Henryvilles, #16 and #18; and Griffith's Gnats and midge emergers, #20 to #24. Hare's Ears or Leadwing Coachmen, #8 to #14, also work well when fished *slowly*, on or near the bottom. While walking on shore or wading near it, watch for sinkholes. These one- to two-foot-diameter depressions (caused by water flows or beaver or muskrat activity) are just deep enough to sprain an ankle or break a leg, and they're usually beautifully camouflaged by grasses, brush, or mud.

An interesting illusion occurs on lake or pond surfaces, especially when they're calm. During a rise, it may appear that trout are rising all over—except where you are. If you run or paddle off to those better waters, you'll witness the same thing: the fish are where you aren't. Your eyes deceive you. In looking out over any broad expanse of water, distant movements appear more prominent than the ones closest to you, the ones you may be overlooking.

Float Tubes

Float tubes (belly boats) not only make lake fly fishing more fun but also more spectacular. The Park Service allows the use of float tubes in waters open to fishing. Imagine floating around a lake at 11,000 feet and looking down through startlingly clear water at cutts and rainbows and then up to snowy peaks and a sky of astonishing blue. It's quite an experience. But getting there is another thing. Without a heavy pack load, a fast-paced hike to Fern Lake can take two hours of hard walking and heavy breathing to cover four miles. At the trailhead, I once met a man returning from the lake carrying a float tube. His trip took six hours one way. So before you try hauling a float tube up to Sandbeach Lake (where, after a 4.5-mile hike and a 2,000-foot elevation gain, you'll find some fine trout), consider hiring a guide to help you make the most of your fishing there, and travel by horseback whenever you can.

Float tubes give you the advantage of greater mobility in the water and more versatility and ease in presentations. As in a real boat, the most significant gain isn't so much in having more water to fish but a better position to fish from. Generally, you should still con-centrate your efforts at the shoreline areas. While trolling from a tube (a very productive technique), limit your line out to sixty or seventy feet. From tube or shore, full-sinking lines are seldom worth the trouble, but sinking-tip ones are.

High lakes can be numbingly cold even in July, so pack in some long johns to wear under your waders.

3

Bugs, Trout Flies, and Their Seasons

A healthy streambed is not just dirt and rock. It's an incredible repository of life, unseen by most, but waiting to surface. When you see a hatch of bugs on the stream, you witness one of nature's greatest wonders. Aquatic insect life thrives in the Park. Major orders are the mayfly, midge, stonefly, and caddis. If you pick up and examine a rock from a Park stream, you'll likely find some of their early life forms, such as a mayfly nymph, midge larva, stonefly nymph, or caddis larva. Some people shake their heads over the weight of my fishing vest and the several fly boxes I carry in it. But after years of fishing the Park, especially in summer, I've learned that on nearly any stretch of water, you might be just as likely in need of a #4 stonefly as a #28 midge or anything in between. The aquatic insects and other trout foods described in this chapter occur commonly in the Park; the recommended imitations have proven highly effective. (A quick note to beginners: Dry flies float and are used to imitate adult insects. Nymphs, sometimes called wet flies, sink. Though inaccurate, the term "nymph" is often used to refer to any early life stage of an insect or to most subsurface flies. Emergers generally ride just below the water's surface.)

Mayfly

The mayfly begins life as a subsurface egg. The egg develops into a nymph, the nymph into an adult dun, a dun into a fully mature spinner. Spinners reproduce, deposit eggs into the water, die,

26

Fig. 3. Mayfly Nymph and Adult

and the cycle repeats. Mayfly metamorphosis is termed incomplete because it moves directly from egg to nymph (skipping larval and pupal stages) to adult. Mayflies range in size from the tiny blue-winged olives (as small as #24) to the much larger *Hexagenia*, over an inch long. The fly angler must be well stocked to match the wide variety found here. An aid in identifying insect types is to observe their flight patterns. A mayfly's flight generally describes smooth, floating arcs.

Sizes: #10 to #24
Colors: Gray, tan, olive, brown, rusty
Hatches: Year-round
Nymph: Pheasant Tail (flashback or plain), Gold-Ribbed Hare's Ear (flashback or plain), Leadwing Coachman
Emerger: Floating mayfly emerger
Adult Dun: Comparadun; standard and parachute versions of Cahill, Adams, Blue-Winged Olive, Hendrickson
Adult Spinner: Flash-Wing Spinner, spinner

Midge

The midge undergoes complete metamorphosis: egg, larva, pupa, adult. The midge is a very small two-winged fly with a dark

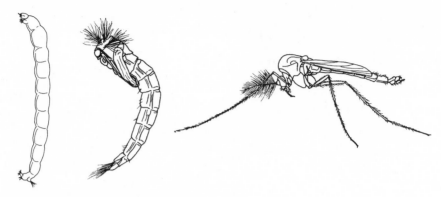

Fig. 4. Midge Larva, Pupa, and Adult

body, disproportionately long legs, and flat transparent wings. Though generally much smaller, it's often mistaken for a mosquito. In flight, a midge tends to alternately hover and bounce up and down.

Sizes: #18 to #28
Colors: Gray, black
Hatches: Year-round
Larva: Midge larva
Pupa: Miracle Nymph
Emerger: Stuck-in-Shuck, Hill's Stillborn Midge
Adult: Griffith's Gnat, Adams

Caddisfly

To the uneducated eye the adult caddis may at first appear to be a moth, but closer examination shows two of the caddis's most prominent features: (1) the wings are not flat, but folded and tentlike; (2) the antennae are long, just about body length, and frequently held pointing backward. Like the midge, the caddis undergoes complete metamorphosis. Many species of caddisfly larvae live within cases, which they build of stone, vegetation, or stream debris and then attach to submerged rocks or branches. A few species of caddis larvae are not case-building but free-swimming. A caddis flight pattern consists of movements that are quick, angular, and often erratic.

Fig. 5. Caddis Larva, Pupa, and Adult

Sizes: #10 to #18
Colors: Tan, brown, light or dark olive
Hatches: March through mid-November
Larva: Gold-Ribbed Hare's Ear, preferably tied on a curved hook
Pupa: Beadhead Soft-Hackle, Caddis pupa
Emerger: Emerging caddis pupa
Adult: Western Coachman, Rio Grande King. Also, Deerhair or Elk-
   hair Caddis, Fluttering Caddis, Parachute Caddis. When more
   "natural" colors fail, try chartreuse, orange, or bright yellow bod-
   ies. For fishing still water, try a Henryville Special with ginger
   hackle. In smaller sizes, hackle may be omitted or trimmed.

Stonefly

An adult stonefly can be confused with an adult caddis, so
watch for two distinguishing characteristics: The stonefly's wings are
held flat, not tentlike, and the antennae are not as long as those of
the caddis. Metamorphosis in the stonefly is incomplete, the two
major life stages being nymph and adult. One of the most common
varieties is the little brown stone, sizes #14 to #16. Hatches of giant
stoneflies occasionally occur, even on tiny mountain creeks. The
adults can measure over 2.5 inches long. An airborne stonefly
moves in a generally linear way with noticeably fluttering wings.

Fig. 6. Stonefly Nymph and Adult

Sizes: #4 to #18
Colors: Tan, dark brown, charcoal, gray
Hatches: Late February through mid-November
Nymph: Prince Nymph, Gold-Ribbed Hare's Ear (flashback), Bird's Stonefly
Adult: Elkhair Caddis, Henryville Special, Sofa Pillow, Stimulator

Damselfly

As an adult, this insect resembles a dragonfly, but the most successfully fished form is the damsel nymph. Damsels are most often found in ponds or lakes (Lily Lake being one example) or in still-water sections of streams. Damselfly metamorphosis, like that of the mayfly and stonefly, is incomplete.

Sizes: #8 to #16
Colors: Olive, gray
Hatches: May through September
Nymph: Damsel nymph. Flies tied with eyes seem to work better than those tied without.

Fig. 7. Damselfly Nymph

Terrestrials

The term "terrestrial" refers to land-dwelling insects such as ants, grasshoppers, crickets, and spiders, which may become trout food when they fall or are blown into the water. You'll see them throughout most of the fishing season. You'll notice a large number of ants in the Park, ranging in size from #14 to #22 and black or cinnamon in color. Foam- or thread-body ants work well on still or moving water. Grasshoppers are fairly common too, even at elevations near 10,000 feet. Size ranges from #8 to #14. Colors are a mix of tan, yellow, and green. Joe's Hopper and the Whitlock Hopper are two fine patterns. In a pinch, use a large caddis. Beetles, crickets, and spiders do not comprise as significant a food source as do hoppers and ants.

Other Fish and Fish Eggs

Once while nymph-fishing the Big Thompson in the canyon, I set the hook on a large rainbow. It appeared to have a foreign object lodged in its mouth, and I determined, if only to assist it, to bring the trout to net. But as I moved the rainbow in closer, it spat out an eight-inch trout (the "foreign object") and swam away. I had missed the subtle take of the smaller fish and unwittingly used it as bait for a larger one. So, apart from the niceties of matching the hatch, remember this: Trout do like to eat fish—and one another!

Don't forget the streamers. The trout's cannibalistic tendency is also revealed in its fondness for trout eggs. Glo-bugs (which some anglers consider unsporting) are spherical fly patterns made of yarn, usually bright orange, green, or a mix of the two colors. They work best on overcast days or in the cold of early and late seasons. Fish them in sizes #12 to #16.

Emergers

Emergence might best be described as the "birth" of an aquatic bug. In its passage to adulthood, the insect rises toward the water's surface and begins to shed its nymphal or pupal sheath. Trout love emergers. They can be more attractive, apparently less labor-intensive targets than the adult forms of aquatic bugs. You may find yourself, for example, in the midst of a mayfly hatch. Trout rise everywhere, and you think you're presenting the perfect artificial—some form of an adult mayfly—but the trout are unimpressed. Chances are that an appropriate emerger would work, so try one. If it doesn't, take a broader view, and reconsider insect type, size, shape, and color.

Size, Shape, and Color of Trout Flies

When you don't have the perfect match for the prevalent bug, or if that match fails, select a fly that most closely approximates, in order of importance, the size, shape, and color of what the trout seem to be eating. Say that adult caddisflies have roused the trout into surface feeding, but your #12 tan Elkhair Caddis gets no attention. You determine that the artificial is too large, so you try one that's a size or two smaller. If that fails, focus your attention on the shape of the natural fly. You might decide that the slimmer profile of a Henryville Special is a better bet. If the Henryville is ignored, take a closer look at the natural fly's color. We'll assume that the insect's abdomen is marked with a spot of bright green. However, the only fly of this color in your possession is a #10 Partridge-and-Green—clearly not an adult caddis imitation and obviously the wrong size. To your surprise, it catches trout. That's an example of the hopeful logic of size-shape-color fly selection.

A couple of quick points regarding size. Choosing a fly that's one size smaller than the natural usually works in your favor. And if, for example, the trout are keyed in on #16 Little Brown Stoneflies but all your perfect imitations are ignored, try a last-ditch strategy: Tie on a #26 ant or a #10 Adams. Fly fishing thrives on the sublime and ridiculous.

Ideal Flies

In the Park, the single best all-round dry fly is a #16 Western Coachman or one of its close relatives: a Rio Grande King or a Trude. This isn't a hard fact, just a widely held opinion among a lot of experienced western fly anglers. The Coachman-style wing (made of calf-tail or calf-body hair) is wonderfully adaptable. To thin it, use a pair of line nippers. Using your fingers and some fly floatant, you can spread the wing out to the sides into a more prominent form. To approximate a mayfly, pinch and pull the wing to a more compact and upright position. You can also fish a Coachman subsurface as an emerger, nymph, or streamer. The Adams (#10 to #20, with regular or parachute hackle) is another great choice for an all-purpose dry fly, and the Stimulator (#12 to #18) can often get fish to strike when nothing else will. The two favorites for nymph fishing are the Gold-Ribbed Hare's Ear (#10 to #16) and the Pheasant Tail (#16 to #22).

Fly Fishing Through the Park Season

The ice-out conditions of early spring demand your patience and versatility. In late February of 1994, for example, I could catch trout on Fall River only with three BB shots pinched onto the tippet about eight inches above a #10 green Hare's Ear. A week later I was alternating between the deep-water rig, a midge emerger, and small dry flies (a #16 Henryville and a #18 Blue-Winged Olive). The adult insects of March through May are generally smaller in size and number than those seen in June through October. The spring months often bring snow and, if you're prepared for it, fly fishing during a snowfall can be a pleasure. The snowflakes on the water may stimulate trout to feed, so you can often use dry flies. In June through early September, the tourist season in the Park reaches its height. Guided horseback trips to high mountain lakes and streams are incomparable. You'll get away from the crowds to fly fishing locations accessible only during the summer months. On lakes, try small caddis and ants on top, Woolly Buggers and other streamers below, and emerging midges and caddis in between. At elevations of 9,000 feet and lower, watch for the big mayfly spinners of late afternoon and early evening. During mornings and afternoons, count on activity from mayflies, stoneflies, and caddis. Unless the weather is unusually warm, don't expect much dry fly fishing until at least 9:30 A.M. September and October (spawning time for browns and brookies) are prime for dry-fly fishing. The trout feed energetically, and multiple hatches of midges, caddis, stoneflies, and mayflies are common. By late October the larger mayflies have mostly disappeared. Midges remain prominent, as do small stoneflies and some surprisingly large (#12) caddis. These conditions persist through ice-in.

Dry-Fly Fishing

Probably the best time for dry-fly fishing in and around the Park is from early July through mid-October. Nearly all major orders of aquatic insects (and most terrestrials) are active, and trout will rise to them. Most of the days will be bright and a bit breezy, with some prolific hatches and marvelous dry-fly fishing. Consider, though, that just one cold night (with sustained temperatures less than 40 degrees) will almost certainly put a damper on surface insect activity the next morning, if not for the entire day. On the other hand, if the weather following a cold night or two is cool and overcast, perhaps with a light rain, you can anticipate some outstanding dry-fly fishing—especially during hatches of mayflies and midges.

Midges and Mayflies

As nearly mature midges and mayflies emerge, the insects remain on the water's surface as they work free from their sheaths, dry their wings, and fly away. It's a rather lengthy process, which helps explain why either hatch can rate among the most enjoyable to fish. Both trout and angler have time and opportunity to capture their respective prey. During a midge hatch, Roger Hill's Stillborn Midge (described in Roger's book, *Fly Fishing the South Platte River*) should be your dry fly of choice. The fly is distinguished by a trailing wispy muskrat shuck as long as the simple thread body. Lightly dress the hackle for a suitably low float and start fishing. Note that Hill's design works subsurface as well. Since most adult midges in the Park are tiny, many of them less than four millimeters long, realize too that an emerging midge can be almost double that size— a more substantial bit of trout food. A Griffith's Gnat sometimes works, but the pattern is best reserved for replicating clusters of mating midges. As thousands of newly hatched bugs blanket the water, using an adult midge pattern is seldom worthwhile. Given a choice, trout nearly always prefer an easy mark: in this case, an emerger stuck in the water, not an adult that might fly off at any moment. Save the Griffith's Gnat and adult patterns for fishing rises to egg-laying midges.

A mayfly hatch is easier to fish if only because you can see the insects better—and there aren't as many of them. A Cahill tied in color and size to match the natural is a favorite Park mayfly imitation. You can present it with exceptional delicacy, it floats well and has good visibility but is not especially wind-resistant. The same pattern is effective also when fished just beneath the water's surface. Quill patterns and the old reliable Adams are two more good choices, though neither makes a convincing impression when fished subsurface. If a floating pattern doesn't work, switch to an emerger. Female adult mayflies return to the water to lay their eggs on or below the surface. Your best bet for a dry fly will be a spent spinner. Subsurface, try a Soft-Hackle.

Stoneflies and Caddisflies

In the Park you may come across caddis hatches so thick that you need to bat the bugs aside just to see around you. And as the water churns with feeding trout, most fly anglers present their best imitation of the adult caddis only to be mystified when trout disregard the dry fly. The question becomes: What happens during a caddis hatch? In its final pupal stage, a caddis might drift beneath the water's surface for several minutes. Then it pops to the surface a full-fledged adult and almost instantly flies away. Naturally, trout prefer a lingering subsurface emerging pupa to a momentarily available adult. Only after the hatch is over do the fish begin to rise in earnest to adult caddisflies. Caddisflies cling to branches or rocks above the water, but their careless flight, a breeze, or both may drop them back onto the currents—then it's dry-fly time.

Dry flies won't work that well during a stonefly hatch, either. Though you may see some airborne or floating stoneflies during the event, most of the trout-feeding action occurs under the water, not on top of it. To shed its nymphal sheath and become an adult, a stonefly leaves the water. Watch for the sheaths, partially split by the emerging adult, on rocks or branches that protrude from the water or along the shoreline. During a stonefly hatch, trout feed most vigorously near these areas—on stonefly nymphs, not adults. Start using a dry fly after the hatch, when adult stoneflies fall or are blown back onto the water. With both caddisflies and stoneflies the best dry-fly fishing of all usually coincides with periods of egg laying, not with hatches. Caddis and stoneflies often deposit their eggs on the water's surface. But some species submerge to lay eggs, in which case the best artificial is usually a Soft-Hackle.

Finding the Right Fly

Even when conditions seem to warrant using a dry fly, don't be stubborn about it. Otherwise, you may miss out on some great fishing opportunities. If a dry fly fails during a hatch, use an emerger; during egg laying, use a Soft-Hackle. Still, rules don't guarantee results. Several years ago in the Park, I couldn't figure out how to fish a hatch of red quill mayflies. I thought I had used every worthwhile imitation and tactic but caught nothing as trout rose around me. I randomly selected a #16 Flashback Gold-Ribbed Hare's Ear, fished it on the surface, and caught one trout after another. The Hare's Ear may have resembled a stillborn, crippled, or shuck-entrapped red quill. It could be that what I thought was a hatch was really a period of egg laying and that the Hare's Ear served as a spent spinner. Or else, heaven forbid, there was no logic to the situation whatsoever and I just got lucky.

Whatever the natural insect may be, determine how high or low, straight or tilted it rides on the water. In short, don't just tie on a fly that matches the natural solely in size and name. Perhaps first you should trim or fluff out parts of dubbed-body flies. Very often, removing some tail fibers is helpful, as is reducing the hackle. You might doctor a dry fly by applying more or less floatant. It may be best to apply no floatant at all—the trout might be more attracted to a fly that's partly submerged. Your observations and actions can determine whether a dry fly fails or succeeds. Once a floating fly gets so waterlogged that false casting doesn't sufficiently dry it, don't just add more floatant. First, dump the fly into a container of dry fly crystals (usually some form of highly absorbent silica or similar substance). Close the lid, shake the container for five seconds or so, and remove the fly. Blow off any excess crystals and false-cast a few times. Then reapply floatant and start fishing again.

Getting a drag-free float on a dry fly is nearly always advisable. Use of a George Harvey leader (described in Chapter 6) helps immeasurably. But what attracts trout one day might bore them the next. Once, while I was fishing a Park lake with a friend, the trout began feeding on flying ants blown down onto the water's surface. I caught trout on nearly every cast; my friend raised none. He let the fly drift freely in theoretically perfect and natural form. In contrast, I made my imitation move a bit by occasionally twitching the rod tip, and that's what piqued the trout's interest. Don't just look at a bug on the water as some little still life. Although aquatic insects may indeed hold themselves motionless as they float atop the currents, quite often they're struggling to leave the water. That's certainly the case with terrestrials like grasshoppers and ants. In the water, hoppers hold stock-still as they drift, but this seemingly peaceful ride is usually interrupted by bursts of frantic activity. And that describes how you should fish your imitation. Caddisflies may skitter around on the water's surface, frequently in opposition to the current. Cast your dry fly downstream and, by successive quick raises of the rod tip, make the artificial "jump" back to you. It's an especially effective technique in fast-moving water and, as you might imagine, lends itself well to fishing tiny brushy creeks.

A Guide to Hatches

The Park doesn't know boundaries. Its wilderness spills over into the Colorado State Forest, the Roosevelt, Routt, and Arapaho National Forests and beyond. Some events in the general area—when the aspen turn, or when bull elk drop their antlers, for example—occur fairly predictably. However, with regard to aquatic insect behavior, I've never known a place as inconstant as the Park, where hatches can occur a month or two earlier or later than anticipated, in greater or smaller numbers. Here's a broad, brief view of Park area hatches: midges and Blue-Winged olive mayflies are a year-round phenomenon; caddisflies and stoneflies usually appear by late February and remain through ice-in. The following chart presents a closer analysis. Remember, though, that it's only a general guide.

Order/Species	Occurrence	Sizes
Blue-Winged olive mayfly	Year-round	#16 to #22
Red quill mayfly	June–September	#14 to #18
Pale morning dun mayfly	June–September	#14 to #20
Green drake mayfly	June–August	#12 to #14
Hexagenia mayfly	June–August	#8 to #12
Little brown stonefly	February–ice-in	#16 to #20
Golden stonefly	June–August	#8 to #16
Giant stonefly	July–August	#6 to #10
Caddisfly	April–ice-in	#10 to #20
Midge	Year-round	#18 to #26
Grasshopper	June–October	#6 to #12
Ant	April–ice-in	#14 to #24

Nymph Fishing

There you are, surrounded by midges in the air and on the water, and trout are feeding everywhere. But the fish refuse all your lovely imitations of midge emergers, adults, pupae, and larvae. Could this be a "masked" hatch, one in which the abundance of one insect disguises the presence of another? Possibly. Look around, on, and in the water for other bugs and see what, if anything, you find. The answer might be in the form of some different order of small adult bugs (little mayflies, for example) flying among and masked by the midges. Or, if you seined the water, you might well discover what you least expected: aquatic insects in early life stages—insects that don't match what's in the air. At nearly any time of day, though most often in early morning and late evening, various nymphs, larvae, and pupae release themselves from their subsurface homes and drift in the currents for a while until they settle down again in a new neighborhood. The drifting period may last from a few minutes to most of an hour. Biologists have verified the behavioral drift phenomenon but can only theorize about why it occurs. Furthermore, the early life forms—larva, pupa, or nymph—of aquatic insects are almost invariably among a trout's favorite foods. So, even a picture-perfect hatch doesn't necessarily show what the trout are eating, and it certainly doesn't always warrant using a dry fly. Your best approach may be nymph fishing.

Casting Weight

Whether a fly floats or sinks doesn't change the nature of water, trout, or presentation. The critical difference between fishing a dry fly and a nymph is weight (within the fly or attached to the leader). Casting a weighted fly in the same way as one would a dry fly usually results in the leader tangling around the rod, so the cast needs to be modified:

1. Open up the range of casting motion to produce wider loops that are less likely to foul the leader.

2. Slow down! Let the line unroll fully and extend— short of hitting the water—at the end of both the back cast and forward cast. The more weight, the slower the cast.

3. Avoid casting with the rod in a vertical position. Keep the rod horizontal to the water and off to your side. (See figure 8; note reel orientation.) You'll get a better view of the line's progress and also avoid hooking yourself.

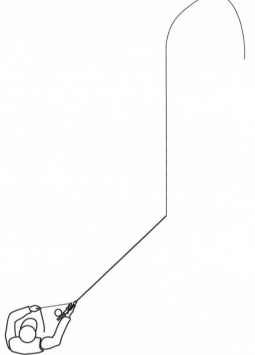

Fig. 8. Sidearm Cast with Wide Loop

Nymphing Indicators

Observing a dry fly's drift is like watching a game of checkers. You can see and anticipate a series of movements taking place on a single plane. With a submerged nymph, the game becomes three-dimensional. How will the nymph travel in relation to the water above, below, and around it? How will you know when a trout has taken the nymph? Ideally, the discernible drift of an indicator will mirror the unseen drift of a submerged fly. An indicator might be the leader itself or some supplemental object attached to it. When an indicator hesitates (no matter how imperceptibly), stops, veers, or vanishes, assume there's a take and set the hook. As a rule, the distance from indicator to fly should be about equal to twice the water's depth. For example, if the water is two feet deep, place an indicator on the leader about four feet from the fly. Especially where waters run low, clear, or calm, keep indicators as inconspicuous to the trout as possible. That's why one of the best indicators to watch, once you develop an eye for it, is simply the leader itself, either untreated or else greased with floatant up to the spot where a supplemental indicator would be placed.

The leader-as-indicator works best in subdued lighting, but the Park's sun produces a lot of water glare. Considering that, two other kinds of indicators work especially well. Fluorescent red strike paste or putty is highly visible, reusable, and buoyant. It's fairly easy to apply putty to a leader: take a tiny pinch of the putty, then press and roll it into place. The putty stays on the leader moderately well, though you can reposition it without much trouble. (It's helpful, too, when fishing tiny dry flies in difficult light conditions.) Three pieces of the putty, each spaced about two inches from the next, create one of the most efficient and sensitive indicator setups possible. Another good indicator is a dry fly: a #14 Parachute Adams or Stimulator works well. Use an improved clinch knot to tie an appropriate length of tippet to the hook bend of the dry fly and the same knot to tie the nymph to the end of the tippet. In this arrangement, the dry fly is termed a "point" fly and the nymph a "dropper" (see figure 9).

One of the best droppers is a #20 Pheasant Tail or a #18 Hare's Ear. Though the dry fly (which should be kept well dressed with

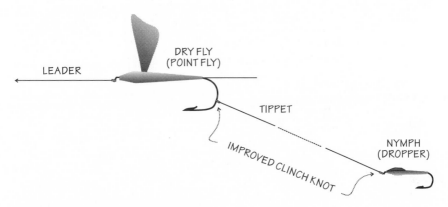

Fig. 9. Dry Fly with Nymph Dropper

floatant) serves mainly as an indicator, it will likely catch a trout or two along the way. You can also rig two nymphs together in a similar manner. A #14 Prince Nymph as point fly and a #16 Flashback Hare's Ear as dropper is a great combination. Use strike putty indicators. Indicators such as adhesive foam or a floating ball/cork are best reserved for use in choppy water that disguises their presence. A short piece of yarn attached to the leader with a slip knot forms a delicate, easy-casting indicator suitable for most water conditions. Whatever indicator you use, remember that trout can take and spit out an artificial fly in less than a second. Because of leader length and slack, a take is not communicated to the indicator at the instant it occurs but a moment later. Therefore, your observation of the indicator must be uncommonly intent and your hook-set quick.

Adjusting Weight and Tippet

When nymphing, use a longer than average tippet (about thirty-five to forty inches suits most situations). It has a bit more give and stretch and helps avoid break-offs. Recommended sizes are 4X to 6X. The closer the weight is to the fly, the faster the fly will sink. Weight placed farther up the leader sinks the fly more slowly but also allows it to swing up (like an emerger or dislodged bug) in its drift through the current. It's seldom necessary to place weight more than two feet away from the fly but often imperative to clinch on a shot right next to the hook eye. Conditions dictate. At times a trout will take artificials only as they bounce along the streambed; at others, nymphs must be drifted at varying levels within the currents. Water depth, current speed, leader length, tippet diameter, and where the fish are feeding are just some of the variables. Adapt or go fishless. For the best results—or any results at all—you'll have to adjust weight, size, quantity, placement, and indicator location nearly constantly—until you discover the magic combination. Only then is it time to move on and start all over again, recalling the rules and hoping for luck.

Weighted Flies

Some anglers maintain that weight tied into a fly (as opposed to weight being clinched onto the tippet) is best, while others claim it prevents a natural appearance. Still others say it doesn't much matter, which is the case in the Park. Even in a small area, stream and river environs can be remarkably diverse. Imagine a run less than ten feet long and two feet deep, the riffle ahead eight inches deep and fifteen feet long, the pool above four feet deep and five feet across. A #14 olive Hare's Ear matches the caddis larvae the trout are eating. While a weighted fly is perfect for the run, it's too heavy for the riffle and too light for the pool. Flies tied unweighted are certainly easier to modify as you fish, and you'd probably prefer adjusting weight to changing flies. Beadhead flies incorporate a brass bead that is slipped over the hook shank and affixed next to the hook eye during tying. Their light weight adapts them well to subsurface fishing of shallows. Add shot and they are productive in deeper waters, too. Why trout are attracted to beads is anybody's guess, but a few of the best proven beadhead patterns are Soft-Hackles, Prince Nymphs, and Hare's Ears. Placing a bead on a Pheasant Tail is gilding the lily.

4

Fish Sense:
Casting and Presentation

The best fly anglers have no magical fly, extraordinary luck, or secret tackle, but all share a highly developed talent for fishing thoroughly and patiently and for presenting a fly naturally and enticingly. They can catch trout, or at least raise them, when and where others cannot. Notably in small, fast waters—the kind found in the Park—the exceptional fly angler might present a fly at a distance of eight feet and hook a trout, while the average fly fisher casts thirty feet and catches nothing. In the Park, a long cast doesn't work as well as a short one. You'll need to concentrate on finesse, not distance.

Most successful presentations are made with no more than ten to fifteen feet of line off the rod tip. That length of line, a leader averaging nine feet long, an eight- or nine-foot rod, and the length of your own arm can cover the better part of thirty-five feet. Seldom should any cast (measured from the angler to the end of the leader) exceed a distance of thirty feet. Many times, an even shorter fly line, or none at all (just the leader), works best. Why? In most places, the currents are twisted and complex, even if they appear simple and straight, and the drift of a fly, no matter how nicely placed initially, will be ruined by the excessive lengths of tackle attached to it. You'll also have to contend with overhanging trees and brush that frequently ensnare trout flies.

Drag and Drift

Trout flies are remarkable little triumphs of human design. Curious anglers discovered long ago that a fly allowed to drift freely (without any tackle attached) catches trout, and I've accidentally spilled enough

44

flies to vouch for that observation. We introduce a problem as old as the sport itself when we tie fly to tippet (and therefore to leader and line): drag. The fly's natural drift is burdened and degraded by the tackle, so a dry fly creates a wake and a subsurface fly moves unnaturally. In either case, the fly no longer attracts trout but repels them. There are several ways to defeat drag, including improved self-position, mending, casting techniques, and special leaders. But the single best drag-defeating device is simply reduction of the amount of line on the water. For an even better drift, reduce the amount of leader and tippet on the water as well: that's where a shorter cast comes in, and often with it, a trout. Always finish every drift. Allow the fly to float through its full course until drag sets in, as it inevitably will. Too many fly anglers, impatient for the next cast or certain that no fish are nearby, will prematurely pull a drifting fly out the water just when a trout is about to grab it, losing not only the opportunity at hand but the many that might have followed. A fly yanked out of a decent drift unsettles trout. The situation is similar to having your favorite entrée repeatedly presented and snatched away by a distracted waiter. You and your companions would be wise to dine elsewhere.

The Fish In Front of You

Once you've settled quietly into your casting area, watch for the fish themselves or their likely locations before you start to cast. You should already have looked for trout (see Chapter 2), but do it again. You'll likely begin to see trout that are less than a rod length away. Most anglers don't take the time to observe but instead cast over the unseen fish right in front of them and then wade on through, scaring away not only those trout but others for yards around. Watch a really good fly angler—or a heron! There is no substitute for observation and patience.

Line and Rod Handling

Countless times fly anglers spot their quarry and make good presentations only to lose control of their line or the fish at the end of it. Immediately after making a cast, always insert the fly line between the index and middle fingers of your rod hand and then, with your other hand, strip the line back in time with the current. The results: an improved drift (since less line stays on the water) and a tighter line, ready for a hook-set.

Try holding the rod high and parallel to the water, sometimes while leaning far forward with your arm fully extended—it's a highly effective technique. A high reaching rod helps cut the water's contact with line, leader, and tippet, further reducing drag and increasing chances of a take. Always point at and follow the course of a fly's drift both with the fly rod and with your body.

Delicacy and Presentations

Not infrequently you'll see people slap and froth the water with their fly lines yet still expect to catch fish. As a rule, delicacy of presentation catches trout, and the exceptions are, well, exceptional. Maybe giant stoneflies or mammoth caddis or clumsy ants or frantic hoppers are splashing onto the water's surface driving the trout into careless and gluttonous feeding, but those times are rare (and cherished). When fly fishing the Park, subtlety and discretion are consistently rewarded, so get in the habit of making your presentations well-considered and quiet.

We all develop habits of which we remain unaware. One of the most common in fly anglers is the tendency, after making a less than ideal presentation, to jerk the line from the water preparatory to another, better cast. This is emotion overriding sense. The angler, disgusted by his or her poor performance, wants to improve on it but overlooks the fact that there are few better ways to scare trout. So, when you make a bad presentation, live with it all the way through the end of its drift. Whenever possible, use an up-and-across presentation. It's the best all-round for dry flies and nymphs. Wind, calm, or glaring sun may demand a down-and-across delivery. (The two techniques are briefly described in the Appendix.)

Regardless of presentation, reducing the visual impact of line and leader is desirable. Since looking into sunlight obscures vision, always try to place line and leader so that they drift by on the sunlit side of a fish; on the other side, their appearance is accentuated. Avoid placing line and leader directly over trout.

Line Mending

You're bound to fish water where currents take quick control of the line and almost immediately the fly begins to drag (see figure 10). In such instances you need to repair, or mend, the line's drift.

Mending requires that you transfer energy to the line through the rod tip. These steps describe how to perform a simple upstream mend:

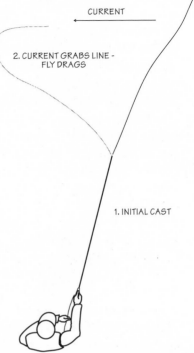

Fig. 10. Current Demands Line Mending

1. Keep a tight line between the grip and stripping guide.
2. Point the rod tip down toward the line in the water.
3. Rotate your wrist and forearm to the downstream side.
4. Sharply and quickly rotate your wrist and forearm to the upstream side.

The line will follow the raised curved motion you should have imparted to the rod tip. A section of line will lift from the water and form an airborne arc that alights pointing upstream (see figure 11).

In this simple form of upstream mending you counteract, or at least forestall, the damage caused by the grab of the downstream current. (If you need to execute a downstream mend, follow the same procedure, but start it from the upstream side.) On Park streams it may be necessary to mend line several times in the course

of one short drift. In addition, it's possible and often
desirable to throw mends
into the leader only. Mending helps defeat drag, and
less drag means more trout.
Refine your skills: A perfect
mend can be as rare and
worthwhile as a perfect
cast.

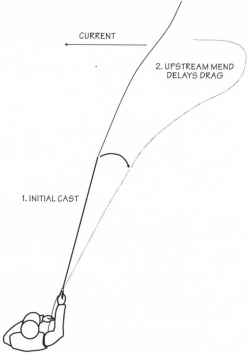

CURRENT

2. UPSTREAM MEND
DELAYS DRAG

1. INITIAL CAST

Fig. 11. A Simple Upstream Mend

Adapting to the Water's Demands

From a presentation
standpoint, riffles and pockets are among the easiest
and most productive types
of water to fish, though
many anglers avoid them, thinking the waters are "too fast." A fly
drifting erratically in the bouncing current of a riffle makes an attractive target to the trout, especially since riffles can mask presentation flaws. In pocket water, concentrate your presentations on just
one pocket at a time. Make short casts (five or ten feet) to suit the
quick, short drifts that follow (often less than a foot). It's a fast, efficient approach called "picking pockets." A run often presents the
challenge of many small complex currents flowing within a dominant one. Fish each current individually and thoroughly.

Pools and flat water can be difficult because their surfaces may
provide little cover to angler or trout. Take advantage of overcast
days, breezes, and low light. Fish methodically, and do your best to
control drag. Often you won't see any trout, just the water you think
holds them. Mentally impose on the water a grid pattern of six- to
twelve-inch squares. It's a scaled-down version of an approach used
by search-and-rescue teams when looking for a person lost in the

wilderness. Begin by drifting the fly through the imaginary grid squares nearest you and gradually work the fly out to the ones farthest away. The method is just as rewarding as it is painstaking.

Consider also the advantages of fishing where other people don't. Water that looks ideal to you may have held the same appeal to many others who have already fished there. But waters that most challenge the angler present the greatest opportunities because they're the most neglected.

Practicing Stealth

Just about any place you fish in the Park, you should do whatever you can to downplay and disguise your presence. Wear dull colors and avoid carrying articles that flash in the sunlight. Voices do not bother trout, but low frequency sounds—the ones you can cause by dragging your feet while wading or by walking and stomping too close to the bank—alarm them. On water or land, stay as low as possible. The higher you stand, especially in relation to deeper water, the easier it is for trout to see you. Casting from a kneeling position may be the only way to catch trout, especially in areas of little cover, bright sun, or both. All casting and line motion should be kept to a minimum. Play and land trout quietly, with little disturbance to the water and other trout around you. Keep the sun at your back or to your side. Make presentations that approach a trout from its sunlit side, but don't let your shadow fall within its view. Use cover like trees, brush, and rocks to hide yourself from the fish. If conditions in a particular piece of water are not conducive to a good presentation, don't fish there. But if you think they will improve later, return then. The lighting of early morning and late evening provides some of the best natural cover to your presence. So do wind, rain, and snow.

DCASTS

Perhaps by now you've surmised that successful fishing in the Park involves being miserable, cramped, unfashionably dressed, and on your knees in ice water in the dark—and what could be more fun? At the least, you'll give your nonfishing friends and family something to smile about. The attributes of the best presentations are summed up by DCASTS: delicate, controlled, accurate, short, thorough, and stealthy. Overlook one element and you won't be doing as well as you might. Get all six going at once and you'll be the one who's smiling.

5

Catching and Releasing

Yes, as everyone knows, meditation and water are wedded for ever.
—Herman Melville

The trout takes the fly and the angler stands by oblivious. I've seen it happen hundreds of times. For beginner or expert, with dry fly or nymph, the sport is by nature extraordinarily visual. If you don't see where the fly is, you can't catch anything with it. You won't see the fly unless you watch it, and you won't watch it unless you concentrate. Concentrate, watch, and see. Too simple a lesson? Think of pro tennis players who hit the ball into the net on an easy volley, or an outfielder who never gets a glove on a routine pop-up. And think of all those trout we've missed. With the myriad distractions in and around Park waters, staying focused isn't easy. But once a fly's in the water, your objective is to see, watch, and concentrate on its drift.

One of the more common "invisible fly" incidents occurs at the end of a cast: you just can't see the fly. Correct this problem by developing and consistently applying a casting discipline. Watch the fly both in the air and as it alights on the water. During a drift, taking your eyes off the fly for even a moment often results in its disappearance. When this happens, you have a couple of options. The most practical is to finish the drift as you search for the fly. Or, like me, you can take an optimistic approach whenever a fly disappears—set the hook. Whatever you do, don't pick up and re-cast; the fly may be over a prime spot that you wouldn't want to disturb.

51

A Hook Set

Setting a hook requires coordination of three elements: attentive vision, good line control, and quick response. Neglect one element and you'll lose a fish. Experienced eastern fly anglers have commented on the phenomenal speed with which western wild trout take and reject a fly. From the moment you see a take, you have less than a second to set the hook, and three problems commonly occur in that brief time. First, anglers become overanxious and actually pull the fly from the trout's mouth. Or, second, they wait too long, and the trout gives up the fly voluntarily. If the timing troubles you, say aloud the word "one" when you see the take—then set the hook. This is not a rigid rule, just a way of enforcing about a one-half second wait between take and set.

The third problem tends to plague anglers who are used to fishing for much larger species like northerns and stripers. They set the hook with power sufficient to propel a little fish out into the trees or to break off their leader on a big trout. The force used to set a hook is about equal to that which goes into a firm handshake. Quickly raise the rod tip about a foot; a tight line and sharp hook will do the rest. Use the same degree of force whenever you set the hook. Though the take of a larger trout is often more subtle than that of a smaller one, you never know what's on until you see it.

Playing a Trout

A good hook-set works commensurately well on a six-inch brookie or a twenty-inch cutt, and any hooked fish merits your total attention. Don't begin to speculate on its size or species. Nonchalance and distraction are unaffordable luxuries. You need to land a trout. Get control of the line! An overly tight line leads to break-offs, a slack one to lost fish. Strip in line until it's taut; as necessary, let it out in the same condition. The angle of rod to water will vary, from near upright initially to pointing downward when a trout jumps. But any rod angle has the same purpose: to help keep the hook in. Even with a small trout on, excess fly line is a nuisance. It can easily foul in water or brush and interfere with a successful landing. Spool up the line as soon as you can and play the fish from the reel. Maintain light contact with the line using two fingers of your rod hand; you may still need to apply extra resistance to outgoing line. A reel's drag should be at its lightest setting short of allowing line overrun.

Catch and Release

Playing a fish for too long exhausts it. The resulting chemical changes in its body can kill it, if not at the moment of landing, then minutes or hours later. Bring in any trout, big or small, as rapidly as you can. In addition, the longer a hooked fish is free in the water, the greater become *your* chances for problems. To expedite landing a trout, use the largest and strongest tippet practical. The smallest you'll need is probably 6X, with 5X a better all-round choice. In relation to the trout's weight, the listed breaking strength of tippet might seem high (for example, 3.5 pounds), but it's quickly diminished by being knotted, tugged, and subjected to the force of currents. Whenever you can, use a landing net, one that's equipped with a cotton bag; nylon is too abrasive. A finely meshed bag won't snag or tear at fins or gills the way a widely meshed one will. A net of very fine mesh (with openings smaller than an eighth of an inch) can double as a seine for collecting bug samples from the water. Since most trout spook at the sight of a submerged net, wait until the trout is within reach before you plunge the net into the water to capture it. Once the fish is netted, you can leave it there until after you remove the hook.

Whether or not a net is used, wet your hands before handling a trout! Dry hands harm its delicate protective outer membrane. Handle a trout firmly but gently, preferably keeping it in the water and in the net. Use one hand (placed an inch or two behind the gills) to cradle and hold the fish. Do not squeeze the fish or get your fingers in its gills. Very often, holding a trout upside down calms it and so greatly eases getting the hook out.

The most familiar difficulty with hook removal comes from not first taking the time to see how the hook entered. Once that's done, back it out the way it went in. Use only barbless hooks. (A fish that bleeds as a result of being hooked usually survives.) When a trout is so deeply hooked as to make the process of hook removal too lengthy or injurious, clip off the tippet as near to the fly as possible. Eventually the hook will rust away or become dislodged.

All trout should be revived before release. Gently cradle the fish so that it's right side up and facing upstream. Rocking the fish from side to side in the current helps it get reoxygenated. Release it after it makes one or two strong efforts to escape. If the fish seems too weak, don't release it, but don't give up, either. Continue your revival efforts until they're successful.

The Importance of Re-Tying

After each fish caught, take the time to check the integrity of both fly and leader. Will the dry fly still float, or the nymph sink? Are there unwanted knots, nicks, or abrasions in the leader? This is the time to remedy any difficulties—before the next trout. One more action is recommended: Take thirty seconds to cut off and re-tie the fly to the tippet. The tippet at its juncture with the hook eye has been stressed, as has the connecting knot itself. Granted, the hook-tippet connection may still be good, but there's a fair chance it's been weakened, so why take the risk? The next trout might break off your fly in two seconds because you couldn't spare half a minute. For the same reasons, it's also good practice to re-tie the fly to the tippet after every thirty casts or so.

Using Debarbed Hooks

To debarb a hook, squeeze down on the barb with a forceps or pliers. Whatever the fly, always use barbless hooks. They have these advantages over the barbed kind:

1. Better penetration. Debarbing increases hook efficiency because a barb is wedgelike and impedes a hook's ability to pierce.
2. Easier removal. Removing a debarbed hook from a fish is quicker and minimizes injury.
3. More safety. Extracting a debarbed hook from your hand, neck, or face is also easier (and less painful).
4. Legal compliance. Not all Park areas require barbless hooks, but you may wander into one that does.

Humane Killing of Trout

A reminder: Many Park waters are restricted to barbless catch-and-release fishing, and the taking of a greenback cutthroat is always illegal.

It may seem odd, in a book that promotes catch-and-release fishing, to find part of it explaining how to kill a trout. With the Park attracting three million visitors a year, people are going to kill fish there, regardless. And if you respect life, how life is taken becomes a matter of concern.

I once saw a man and child in the Park walking back to their car, the man carrying a good-sized brown trout that was still alive, a forked stick through its gills. He opened the car trunk, tossed the fish in a paper sack, and closed the trunk on both. It was a cruel act, and I told him so. He had planned to kill the trout (which was slowly suffocating) when he got home an hour later. I convinced him to kill it immediately, explained how, and he did.

Severing a trout's spinal column is the quickest and most humane way to kill it. Grip the fish, its belly side down in your palm, in one hand. With the other hand, bring a heavy dull-edged object down very fast and very hard at the base of the fish's skull where it connects to the spine. (A large retracted folding knife works, as does the narrow edge of a small steel pry bar.) If you've done it right the first time, the fish will convulse briefly and die; you'll see a pronounced depression (indicating a severance) where the backbone was attached to the head. If you did it wrong, do it again and get it right.

Better yet, don't kill the trout you catch, just let them go. Wild fisheries are growing more rare and environmentally significant, and catch-and-release fishing helps perpetuate them. In many fisheries that are not wild, catch-and-release practices can help restore them to a self-sustaining state. Returning fish to the water also gives that many more opportunities to other anglers, who in increasing numbers believe that catch-and-release makes the best sport.

6

Gearing Up: Fly Fishing Equipment for the Park

Fly Rods

If you had to use just one fly rod in the Park, a nine-foot, 4/5-weight would be best all around. (The 4/5 designation indicates that a rod is suitable for use with either a double-taper 4-weight line or a weight-forward 5-weight line.) In general, the line weight of a Park fly rod should be between 2 and 6; the rod will be of moderate action and eight to nine feet long. Though Park streams are small, avoid using rods shorter than seven and a half feet; longer rods allow greater control of drifts.

For the past several years, the trend in designing rods has been to make them stiffer, faster, and farther-casting, which contributes nothing to fishing small waters. Fortunately, a few major manufacturers continue to produce at least some models of relatively soft and slow graphite fly rods that are easy to cast and fun to fish, though nothing compares to a fine cane rod. (If you are fortunate enough to have one, use it.) Quality fiberglass rods such as those Fenwick, Orvis, and Shakespeare made during the 1960s and 1970s perform beautifully. If you own a fly rod that's too stiff and fast (a common problem), increase its line weight by one or two sizes. The heavier line will slow down the rod and make short casts easier.

Reels and Lines

The near-perfect trout reel is the Orvis CFO III. Of a different style but of comparable quality are two Hardy models: the Featherweight and the Flyweight. All use spring-and-pawl drags; there's no need for disc drags or multipliers.

The favorite lines are double-taper and floating: Cortland 444 and Orvis Spring Creek. The 444 is best; it's very supple and an excellent performer through a wide range of temperatures. The Spring Creek has a slightly harder finish and shoots line a bit more easily. In line weights 4 and above, the Wulff triangle-taper floating line is another good choice. Fly line color has never seemed to matter in Park waters. Superhard finish "extra distance" lines are not recommended. They tend to coil and kink after repeated short casts as well as during periods of low temperature (below fifty degrees Fahrenheit). They don't wear well, either.

Leaders

Leaders are probably the single most important, and neglected, connection between you, the fly, and the trout. Fly line loop-to-leader connectors are too bulky for delicate presentations and tend to catch in the rod guides. Use a nail knot (or better yet, a Tie-Fast or Easy-Tie tool) to secure a 10-inch length of 25-pound test fluorescent Amnesia monofilament to the fly line. On the water, the Amnesia mono makes your leader easier to see and can also serve as a strike indicator. Tie the leader to the mono with a blood knot. To help the line-leader knot connection slip through the guides, coat it with Aquaseal or a similar waterproof cement. In commercially made leaders, pay special attention to the diameter of the leader's butt end (the part that attaches to the fly line). Leader butts of .015 inch to .022 inch are appropriate to line weights 2 through 6. A leader hyped because of a larger butt is best for heavier lines and bigger fish.

Tippet (high-quality level monofilament) comprises the last 25 percent or so of a mass-produced leader. On a nine-foot leader, that would work out to about twenty-seven inches. Here's a good way to extend the life and versatility of a knotless leader. When the leader is new, cut off the tippet section and save it. Tie a perfection loop in the end of the leader and another in the tippet. Join the loops with a loop-to-loop connection. You'll always know when your tippet section becomes too short, and you'll never again cut back too far into the leader. Use a surgeon's knot or blood knot to tie a new section of tippet onto the old one. When the tippet becomes hopelessly short, tangled, or abraded, remove it and cut a new length of tippet. Tie a perfection loop at its end; reattach it to the leader. You can also prepare preknotted lengths of tippet in the same way before you're on the water.

Braided leaders are marketed under the pretext that they cast more efficiently, which in some ways they do. However, they mend poorly and, unless regularly treated with floatant, splash water while being cast.

The George Harvey Leader

A knotted leader is excellent for fishing most Park waters. Use the knots as visible reference points, especially when fishing subsurface flies. Assuming you know the diameters of its components, a knotted leader is easily repaired or modified in the field.

One of fly fishing's most prominent figures is George Harvey, of State College, Pennsylvania, and he has designed the best trout leader around. Harvey's design combines hard, stiff monofilament (such as Mason) in the leader's lower part with soft, pliable mono (such as Dai-Riki) in the tip section. The tippet length must be altered according to the wind resistance of the fly being cast. A too-short tippet will straighten; one that's too long will pile up. When properly adjusted, the tippet will lay out on the water in S-shaped curves, as will the other soft mono sections. The result: longer drifts, less drag, and more trout.

The drag-defeating characteristics of the leader also allow you to use a stouter tippet than you might otherwise so that you can bring more fish to net more quickly. To take full advantage of the design, perform a kind of check cast: execute your forward-cast delivery about a foot higher than usual, then lower the rod to its normal fishing position.

These leaders have been proven over many years, but they're not available commercially. You'll have to tie them yourself. Here are the components and lengths for an approximately eight-and-one-half-foot 5X Harvey leader:

Hard Monofilament		Soft Monofilament	
Diameter	Length	Diameter	Length
.015-inch	12 inches	.008-inch	12 inches
.013-inch	12 inches	.007-inch	18 inches
.011-inch	12 inches	.006-inch	22 to 30 inches (tippet)
.009-inch	8 inches	—	—

Tie each section to the next with a blood knot, using just three or four turns per knot for the heavier sections and five turns for the lighter ones. Join the final piece of .007-inch nylon to the .006-inch 5X tippet with two perfection loops in a loop-to-loop connection.

If you need a finer tippet, do not completely remove the original tippet section—always leave at least ten inches intact. Then tie on an appropriate length of tippet that is one or two X sizes smaller.

A quick note: Especially when joining different brands of monofilament, always check knot integrity.

Here are two more Harvey leader formulas.

Approximately ten-foot 4X:

Hard Monofilament		Soft Monofilament	
Diameter	Length	Diameter	Length
.015-inch	20 inches	.009-inch	12 inches
.013-inch	20 inches	.008-inch	18 inches
.011-inch	20 inches	.007-inch	22 to 30 inches (tippet)

Approximately twelve-foot 5X:

Hard Monofilament		Soft Monofilament	
Diameter	Length	Diameter	Length
.015-inch	20 inches	.008-inch	12 inches
.013-inch	20 inches	.007-inch	18 inches
.011-inch	20 inches	.006-inch	22 to 30 inches (tippet)
.009-inch	12 inches	—	—

A Detailed List of Equipment

What you wear and carry is as important as your rod, reel, line, and terminal tackle. This is a nearly complete list of what I use while fly fishing the Park, whether I'm guiding or fishing alone. First, neoprene or Gore-Tex chest waders, with wading safety belt. You can wade most waters with hip boots, but they prevent kneeling in the water and negotiating deep areas. When you fall in, the elastic belt (which also carries a clip-on canteen) prevents water from ever reaching your legs. I usually wear my waders rolled down to waist level. Then, studded, felt-soled wading boots are a must. There's nothing better for sure footing on ice, slippery rocks, submerged mossy logs, and while hiking.

Here's what's in or on the vest, beginning with items for safety, survival, and comfort:

Space blanket	Ten-foot length of rope
Waterproof matches	Flashlight; spare batteries and bulbs
Compass	Map
Whistle	Rain jacket
Socks	Bandanna
Tissues	Granola bars
Lip balm	Sunscreen
Bug repellent	Aspirin

Specific fly-fishing items:

Line nippers	Two pair forceps (one is a spare)
Swiss Army knife	Tie-Fast knot tyer
Hook sharpener	Landing net
Small scale	Fleece fly patch
Paste fly floatant	Dry-fly crystals
Leader sink (mud)	Line-cleaner pad
Spare leaders	Tippet, sizes 2X to 7X
Split shot, micro to BB	Indicator putty, foam, corks, and yarn

I also carry eleven fly boxes, four of which contain midge adults, larvae, and emergers. The other seven hold Blue-Winged Olives, Cahills, Comparaduns, spinners, caddisflies, stoneflies, nymphs, streamers, wet flies, and terrestrials. I begin a trip with one vest pocket empty and use it for packing out trash.

Of course, there are the fly rods. I take three or four and select one on-site—usually an eight-foot 2-weight, a nine-foot 3-weight, an eight-foot 4/5-weight (all two-piece models), or a four-piece nine-foot 6-weight. Along with them go some reels and extra, line-loaded spools. Back in the car there are a few sets of dry clothing, towels, gloves, sweatshirts, toilet paper, drinking water, seventeen pounds of gravel, a complete set of *National Geographic* dating back to 1938, and an anvil.

7

Destinations:
Some of the Park's Finest

T his chapter lists the Park's premier fly-fishing destinations with comments on each, and includes a reference map. A few notes are in order first. Reach the east side of the Park via U.S. Route 36 from Boulder or U.S. Route 34 from Loveland. You'll arrive in the town of Estes Park, a year-round community of about five thousand residents and many hotels, restaurants, and shops. Signs will direct you to the main Park entrances: Beaver Meadows (on U.S. Route 36) or Fall River (on U.S. Route 34). Trail Ridge Road is the most direct route to the Park's West Slope, but it's open only part of the year, usually from the end of May until October depending on weather conditions. Alternately, follow Interstate Route 70 west from Denver to U.S. Route 40 west to Grand Lake. This little West Slope town (population approximately 250) on the Park's southwest corner offers lodging and services mainly during the summer.

Keep current with Park fishing regulations, available at Park Information Centers. Wherever you fish in Colorado, greenback cutthroats, if hooked, must always be immediately returned to the water unharmed. Don't be misled by what seems a "short" distance to a destination. Hiking a steep Park trail is very slow and often painful going—at best you'll make about a mile or two an hour. *Always* take along a good (USGS) topo map of the Park. If you choose a destination that's more than a four-mile hike in, plan on camping, traveling by horseback, or both. Camping is allowed only in designated areas and with permits available from the Park Service. Shuttle buses

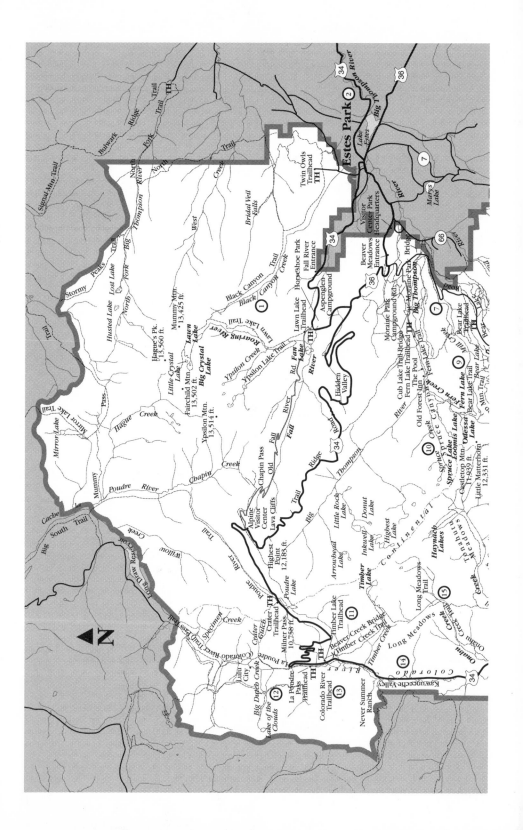

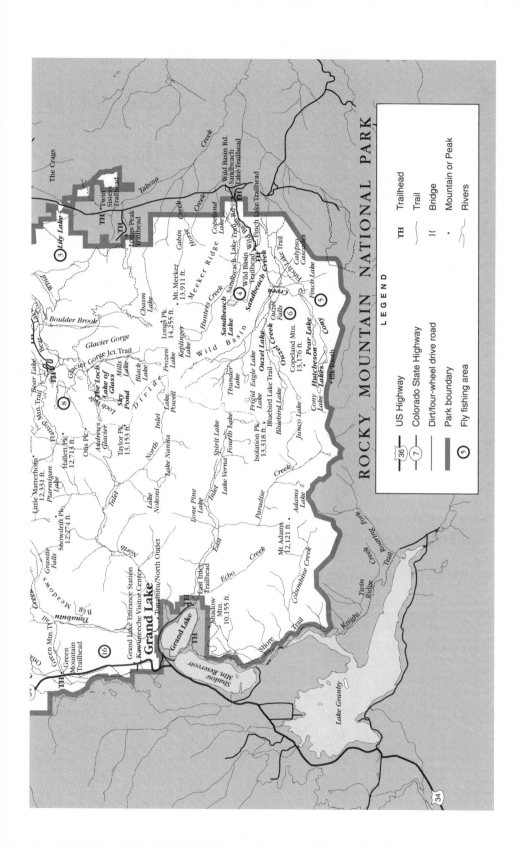

ROCKY MOUNTAIN NATIONAL PARK

LEGEND

36 — US Highway	**TH** Trailhead
7 — Colorado State Highway	---- Trail
...... Dirt/four-wheel drive road	)(Bridge
▬▬ Park boundary	• Mountain or Peak
5 Fly fishing area	~ Rivers

are available to and from many trailheads, and some livery stables in the Park provide horse rental and wrangler services.

Regarding fishing guides and horse wranglers: What you pay isn't what they get. Guides and wranglers usually receive a small percentage (if any) of your fee. They depend on your tips for income; consider tipping at least 15 percent of what you've paid up front. The cost of any special services rendered—food, instruction, gear, clothing, and so on—usually comes out of the guide's or wrangler's own pocket, so you may want to take that into account as well.

Thanks to the Park Service, the East Slope holds many more accessible populations of greenback cutts than does the West Slope. West Slope trail systems aren't as numerous or well developed as those on the East Slope, so West Slope waters are generally harder to reach. Those are the two main reasons why East Slope fly-fishing destinations outnumber their West Slope counterparts. At the same time, the Colorado River and its surrounding waters could encompass a dozen East Slope creeks. A large section of this chapter is devoted to Grand Lake fly fishing, on the West Slope.

In the following descriptions, "Miles" is the one-way distance to a destination. "Hike" indicates the degree of hiking difficulty, a rating based on round-trip mileage, elevation gain, terrain, and trail conditions.

Big Thompson River, Moraine Park

Access: Bear Lake Road bridge over Big Thompson River (Area 7); elevation 8,100 feet
Miles: Roadside
Species: Brown, brook, rainbow, greenback cutt
Regulations: Rocky Mountain National Park

Most of this area is mountain meadow. Apart from grasses and an occasional alder, there's little cover along the banks, so you'd best keep a low profile. Plan on casting from a kneeling position and moving in a crouch. When fishing thin, spooky sections, make your presentations from a distance of at least twenty feet from the banks.

Besides the smooth glassy stretches, there's plenty of water variety: undercut banks, pools, riffles, runs, and backwaters. The big undercuts hold special fascination. I remember trying to probe the depth of one with a nine-foot fly rod; the submerged rod never did touch bank or bottom. The whole area is great habitat for all trout, though browns and brookies seem to do best there, probably because the Moraine waters get so much exposure to the sun.

As you wander through the grasses, you may come across old farm tools, crockery shards, and fence posts, all remnants of a community long gone. Though today it's hard to conceive of, as recently as the 1920s the Moraine held an entire town, complete with golf course. On the south side of the Moraine, twenty or so private residences still stand, and most are still occupied, if only during the summer season. And though they're within the Park, these are still private properties—no trespassing allowed. Fortunately for the angler, the best fishing is on the Moraine's north side. So are the best insect populations.

It's the caddis that really warrants attention. Imitations of all caddisfly life phases are vital to fly-fishing success in the Moraine. When all else fails, try a caddis larva fished deep; brown or black leech patterns often produce when nothing else will, especially in the riffles. Midges and mayflies have a prominent presence, too, as does the little brown stonefly. Concentrate your efforts from the bridge at Bear Lake Road upstream to the footbridge at the Cub Lake Trail.

Big Thompson River, U.S. Route 34 Canyon

Access: U.S. Route 34 east, below Lake Estes dam (Area 2); elevation 7,300 feet
Miles: Roadside
Species: Rainbow (stocked) and wild brown
Regulations: State of Colorado and as posted

Though it's outside Park boundaries, flowing mostly through Roosevelt National Forest along U.S. Route 34, the Big Thompson River originates in the Park. The river offers excellent fishing from the Lake Estes dam downstream past the town of Drake.

One of my fly-fishing neighbors, Travis, is a third-generation Coloradan and now about eighty years old. Once, in 1989, we talked about the Big Thompson River in the canyon. I told him of its fine fishing, but he was dubious, being more than old enough to recall the river long before a devastating 1976 flood. Caused by torrential rains, the flood killed scores of people and wasted much of Estes Park and nearby communities. It also scoured and reformed the Big Thompson River below the Lake Estes dam. Before the flood, anglers like my neighbor rightly considered the Thompson one of the state's top trout fisheries, but afterward the river seemed a lost cause. I assured him that the fly fishing was terrific now—lots of trout, lots of insects. A bit less skeptical, Travis asked, "Ever use stoneflies there?" Yes, I said, they work great. Before I could talk about how I fished them, he smiled and said, "Hard to catch, aren't they?"

If you're new to the sport, not old enough to remember, or both, my neighbor's remark referred to the practice of collecting and then fly fishing with live bait: nymphs, grubs, worms, fish eggs, minnows—any natural, suitable subsurface "lure" that could be caught, cast, and drifted. Today, golden stoneflies and little brown stoneflies remain a significant part of Big Thompson trout food. However, about a five-mile stretch of the river between the Estes Gun Range bridge downstream to the Waltonia bridge is restricted to artificial fly or lure and is catch-and-release only—no live stonefly nymphs allowed.

The river has indeed rebounded from the 1976 flood. About a third of the trout caught in this stretch of the Big Thompson are wild browns, the rest stocked rainbows. Downstream of the Waltonia bridge on through the town of Drake there are no special regulations in effect. Much of the river is steep and full of pockets, plunge pools, and narrow runs—fast, fun fly fishing.

From the dam down to the bridge the river is a hybrid of freestone and tailwater. In the winter, water released from the dam barely keeps more than about a half-mile of a shallow, exposed stretch of the river from freezing over. At the same time, the insect life is what you'd expect in a good tailwater: plenty of Blue-Winged olive mayflies and midges, and lots of stoneflies and caddisflies, too. A #14 Prince Nymph with a #16 Flashback Hare's Ear dropper is one of the most effective subsurface combinations.

The trout often move from one part of the river to another, so take extra care to spot fish before you begin casting. Watch for private property signs, too. From June through August the river gets fished pretty heavily. Out of respect to the river, the sport, and the trout, you might want to consider other destinations during that time.

Fall River

Access: U.S. Route 34 and Endovalley Road (Area 1); elevation
8,500 feet
Miles: Roadside
Species: Brown, brook, rainbow, greenback cutt
Regulations: Rocky Mountain National Park

Just six years after the Big Thompson flood, an earthen dam at Lawn Lake gave way during heavy July rains. A thirty-foot-high wall of water crashed down the mountain through Roaring River. The water passed through Fall River in the Horseshoe Park wetlands but still packed power sufficient to wipe out lodges along Fall River Road, to flood downtown Estes Park, and to kill at least one camper (another was never found)—miles from the site of the breached dam.

At the time, Lawn Lake water, though within Park boundaries, was privately controlled and "maintained." In 1982, the legally declared assets of the Lawn Lake water organization could barely cover the cost of a broken window in downtown Estes Park. Beyond any recompense was life lost, habitat destroyed, and businesses ruined. You should know that, to this day, National Parks are *not* fully protected, and that their exploitation poses a real and on-going threat to all of us.

By all expert accounts, Fall River died in 1982. A 1986 environmental study predicted that normal insect and fish life might not return for generations. The report stated that the only insects present in Fall River were blackflies, and that there was no sign of trout. I'm grateful that fish and bugs can't read. Four major orders of aquatic insects (caddis, stones, mayflies, and midges) have reappeared. You can catch trout again—wild browns, brookies, rainbows, greenback cutts, cuttbows, and stocked rainbows. In 1995, Fall River is coming back stronger than ever. Most often, though, you just can't see trout in postflood Fall River. The river is still stabilizing, and particulates load what seems perfectly clear water. I remember stubbornly fishing a two-foot-diameter pocket in Fall River a couple of years ago, confident it held at least one trout. More than thirty presentations later, I'd hooked and landed a ten-inch brown. Of course, not all Fall River fly fishing is so arduous, but it's often baffling. Don't give up.

In the meadows of Horseshoe Park the river demands as much delicacy and finesse as does a spring creek. The surface is smooth and there's minimal cover: some undercut banks, overhanging grasses, and a few alders. The slightest angler error scatters trout for yards around; you'll have to wait at least twenty minutes for things to settle down again. Use a twelve-foot leader tapering to 6X and a rod no heavier than a 4-weight. Unless the weather's inclement, the best times to fish there are around dawn and dusk.

A few hundred yards upstream of Aspenglen Campground, Fall River becomes pocket water. The fishing is much faster and less demanding than that of the meadow. Browns, brookies, greenback cutts, and rainbows there have all been known to fall for a #12 Parachute Adams floated through a Fall River run.

Roaring River

Access: Lawn Lake Trailhead (Area 1); elevation 8,500 feet
Miles: 1.5

Hike: Moderate to slightly difficult
Destination elevation: 9,300 feet
Species: Greenback cutt
Regulations: Catch-and-release, barbless single hook, artificial only
Camping: Yes
Horse trail: Yes

Roaring River, one of the Park's best and most overlooked fisheries, is another story of a water's death and rebirth. Ravaged and scoured by the 1982 flood, there seemed little hope for the river's revival, but several years later the Park Service planted greenback cutts there. Today the cutts flourish: a healthy, self-sustaining, and, apart from a stray rainbow, exclusive population. In 1994 I guided a Pennsylvania couple, Bob and Terry, on Roaring River. Their trip in many ways typifies a Roaring River fishing experience and Park fishing in general.

First, remember that both of them are far above average fly anglers, with close ties to the remarkable Pennsylvania fly-fishing community. Both have fished nearly all over the world, though this was their first high-mountain trek.

The Lawn Lake Trailhead is at an elevation of about 8,500 feet. Trail distance is 1.5 miles, and the destination elevation is roughly 9,300 feet. The eight-hundred-foot difference between starting and ending points is termed elevation gain. In everyday language, it's pretty damned steep. For every half-mile you walk, you go up 267 feet, about the length of a football field—one that's narrow, twisted, tilted, and covered with loose rock and dirt. If that doesn't sound tough, factor in oxygen-poor air. Not all the trail is consistently mean; it's tempered by curves and switchbacks. Even so, the Pennsylvanians had their work cut out for them, and our trip, counting frequent five- and ten-minute breaks, took over two hours. (Partway up his first hike there, and still in view of the parking lot, one of my friends said, "This is the first time I've walked a mile to go a hundred feet.") Watch for the turnoff and bridge to the Ypsilon Lake Trail. The river fishes best from there on upstream. The nearest camping area is at Ypsilon Creek, about a mile up Roaring River on the west side.

In places, Roaring River is almost narrow enough to jump across, so wading isn't necessary. However, my clients had insisted on using short (six- to seven-foot) rods. Despite the smallness of the fast-moving water, nine-footers would have worked far better. The cutts usually hold in the pockets, a situation that dictates short, controlled drifts, often with just a few inches of leader touching the water. A Stimulator or caddisfly with a dropper works well, as does nearly any stonefly or caddis nymph. Grasshoppers appear by mid-July. However, Bob and Terry both began fishing with long casts and caught no trout. Once their flies hit the water, drag set in almost instantly because of the excessive lengths of line and leader left to merciless currents. To fish here successfully, I explained, work a short line, hold the rod high, and extend your arm. Once they followed the advice, both began to catch fish, though the short rods still couldn't give them much of a reach advantage.

Technique aside, just staying on your feet here poses serious problems. Because of the 1982 flood, the banks of Roaring River are probably the most unstable and troublesome of any water in the Park. Even the largest and most secure-looking rock might flip or roll under the slightest pressure. Every step should be taken with care, and every handhold, too. After a few hours of good fishing, storm clouds and thunder moved in from the north. The terrain around Roaring River is essentially a boulderfield, and the nearby woods are pretty thin. It's not the best place to ride out a thunderstorm, though I've been caught in several there, and spent anywhere from twenty minutes to an hour huddled up in some brush along the west bank. Though the weather did look ominous, I sensed it would blow around us, which, as it turned out, it did. Nevertheless, the clouds and thunder rightly spooked my clients, who insisted on leaving immediately. About ten minutes into our hike back to the car, Bob and Terry learned that going down the mountain—a knee-pounding, sweaty balancing act—could be as uncomfortable and lengthy as the way up. Plans for the next trip included a wrangler and some horses.

The Loch, Sky Pond, Lake of Glass

Access: Glacier Gorge Junction Trailhead (Area 8); elevation 9,200
      feet
Miles: 3
Hike: Easy to moderate
Destination elevation: 10,200 feet
Species: Cutt, rainbow, cuttbow, brook
Regulations: Rocky Mountain National Park
Camping: Yes
Horse trail: No

The Glacier Gorge Junction Trail is one of the Park's most popular and heavily traveled, not so much by anglers as by tourists in
general and photographers in particular. About 1.5 miles from the
trailhead, watch for and take the west fork to Loch Vale. The east
fork goes toward Mills Lake, a pretty water that holds rainbows. The
destination for most folks is Alberta Falls, only about a half-mile up
from the trailhead. After that, the foot traffic thins out.

All the Park's lakes are beautiful, but The Loch is exceptionally
so. From its south end you'll see Cathedral Wall on the west side of
the water. Behind you and to the west is icebound Andrew's Glacier at nearly 12,000 feet. Wherever you stand, views overwhelm.
Once, while fishing there, I was intent on playing a nice cuttbow
when I became aware of odd clicking and buzzing sounds from behind me. Keeping a tight line on the trout, I glanced over my shoulder to see more than a dozen photographers, all focused on
capturing the scene of a mountain fly angler. The event resembled
a weird press conference. I have a theory that if you fish in the Park
long enough, your photograph will eventually appear in one of
those calendars given away by insurance companies and gas sta-
tions.

Nothing stops photographers, but bug repellent helps keep
away The Loch's mosquitoes. Insect life there is extraordinary.
Though fishing above 10,000 feet, you'd swear the bug activity cor-
responded to an elevation at least a mile lower. Midges, mayflies,

and caddis appear with surprising frequency; stonefly activity is relatively scarce. The midges range in size from #28 to #16; blue-winged olive and red quill mayflies from #26 to #16; and tan or gray caddisflies from #18 to #14.

Yet another delight of The Loch is sight-casting to rising trout. When I travel there, I usually carry two rods: a 3-weight for delicate presentations and a 6-weight for bucking the wind—a pretty typical and worthwhile setup for any Park lake. If you have the time, explore Sky Pond. It's about two miles south and west of The Loch along the same Glacier Gorge Junction trail. En route just a few hundred yards north of Sky Pond, Lake of Glass fishes well for brookies and cuttbows. An eleven-acre water, the secluded Sky Pond has some great fishing for numerous small brookies and an occasional cuttbow.

Fern Lake, Odessa Lake, Spruce Lake, and Loomis Lake

Four of the Park's best greenback lakes, Fern, Odessa, Spruce, and Loomis, lie within a mile of one another off the Fern Lake Trail. All were closed to fishing for several years as greenback populations took hold, and all reopened within just the past few years. In many ways, the techniques, patterns, and observations that apply to Fern Lake are models for the other three waters. Unless you're in a great rush, each lake is worthy of at least a full day's attention.

Fern Lake and Fern Creek

Access: Fern Lake Trailhead (Area 10); elevation 8,200 feet
Miles: 4
Hike: Moderate to slightly difficult
Destination elevation: 9,500 feet
Species: Greenback cutt
Regulations: Catch-and-release, barbless single hook, artificial only

Camping: Yes
Horse trail: Yes

As recently as 1985 Fern Lake was closed to fishing as its green-backs grew to become truly wild, self-sustaining trout. A few years later, when the lake reopened, I was overcome. Cutts were visible nearly everywhere, cruising or rising. I couldn't select a fly or tie a knot, and for most of an hour I was just too amazed to execute a decent cast.

Covering about nine acres and over thirty-five feet deep, Fern Lake is still an exciting place—lots of fish in a glorious setting. Look around and you'll see the Little Matterhorn rising to the south and Gabletop Mountain to the west, both snowcapped even in mid-July. Look into the clear water and you'll see the greenbacks. Unless you're one jaded fly angler, anticipate at least some initial coordination loss on your first trip to Fern Lake.

Favorite flies are midges, caddis, small Blue-Winged Olives, and ants. You'll have plenty of opportunities for sight-casting to cutts, especially those feeding near the shoreline. The inlet side of Fern Creek flows in from Lake Odessa, a little more than a half-mile away and about five hundred feet higher. The creek is small, quick, and brushy, demanding short drifts with large (#10 to #14) dry flies or nymphs. The creek trout aren't fussy, but they are fast.

On your trip up to Fern Lake, allow at least two hours for the hike. Though the Big Thompson River parallels part of the trail, it doesn't fish nearly as well as the Moraine section of the river. Save your energy for hiking. You'll need it, especially during the last half of the trip, which seems endlessly steep. Plan a break near The Pool (which will take about fifty minutes to reach) or at the site of the Old Forest Inn, about ten minutes beyond.

Odessa Lake

Access: Bear Lake Trailhead (Area 9); elevation 9,500 feet, or Fern
      Lake Trailhead (Area 10); elevation 8,200 feet

Miles: 4 via Bear Lake Trailhead or 4.5 via Fern Lake Trailhead
Hike: Moderate to difficult
Destination elevation: 10,000 feet
Species: Greenback cutt
Regulations: Catch-and-release, barbless single hook, artificial only
Camping: Yes
Horse trail: Yes

If you're doing a day-trip hike, choose the Bear Lake Trail. The extra half-mile and elevation gain you'll save over the alternate route will be worth it. If you're camping or on horseback, choose the less-used Fern Lake Trail. Fern and Odessa Lakes are not only close geographically, but both share remarkably similar size, shape, and depth.

Spruce Lake

Access: Fern Lake Trailhead (Area 10); elevation 8,200 feet
Miles: 4.7
Hike: Moderate to difficult
Destination elevation: 9,700 feet
Species: Greenback cutt
Regulations: Catch-and-release, barbless single hook, artificial only
Camping: Yes
Horse trail: No

The four-acre, ten-foot-deep Spruce Lake seems almost intimate when compared to Fern or Odessa. Don't let Spruce's small size mislead you—the fishing can be as good or better than that of its larger neighbors. Both the lake's inlet and outlet waters (southern branches of the main Spruce Creek) are added bonuses. Should you decide to follow the outlet down to Spruce Creek, you'll find even more good fishing there. Words of caution regarding Spruce Canyon through which the creek flows: It's often easier to get down into the canyon than it is to get back up out of it. Proceed slowly and thoughtfully, always thinking of your return route.

Since the Spruce Lake area has camping and horseback access, it's an ideal base for trips to Loomis Lake, about a half-mile upstream and southwest.

Loomis Lake

Access: Fern Lake Trailhead (Area 10); elevation 8,200 feet
Miles: 5.3
Hike: Moderate to difficult
Destination elevation: 10,200 feet
Species: Greenback cutt
Regulations: Catch-and-release, barbless single hook, artificial only
Camping: No
Horse trail: No

Loomis Lake brings you in even closer to the crags of Gabletop Mountain to the west. Nearly the same in surface area as Spruce Lake, Loomis is a bit deeper, about fifteen to twenty feet, and tends to hold slightly larger cutts. If Loomis Lake fishing seems slow, turn your attention to its stretch of outlet creek.

Fan Lake

Access: Endovalley Road (Area 1); elevation 8,500 feet
Miles: Roadside
Species: Brook
Regulations: Rocky Mountain National Park
(*Note:* Runoff in 1995 destroyed many of Fan Lake's banks which may cause the lake to revert to a wetlands. Call the Park Service before going there.)

On the edge of Horseshoe Park to the west of Roaring River, the 1982 floodwaters formed a new pond, originally called Godbolt Lake or Flood Lake and now known as Fan Lake. Shortly after Fan Lake's formation, the water held a high number of brown trout, but today brookies dominate. As you stand on Fan Lake's shore during an evening rise, the lake's surface looks and sounds as if it's being pelted with raindrops. (You can get quite a panoramic view of this phenomenon as you come down the Lawn Lake Trail from Roaring River.) Biologists expect that Fan Lake will pretty much disappear within forty years or so as its bottom gradually fills with silt and plant life. In the meantime, fishing for brook trout there is just fine, usually peaking around dusk. A #16 or #18 parachute caddis is one of the best choices in a dry fly, and similarly sized Soft-Hackles work well subsurface. Since this is a popular, easily accessible area, you may want to try float tubing—for good fishing and to get some distance away from landbound tourists. To the lake's south and west you can see sections of Trail Ridge Road running through the high country.

Another area of Fan Lake that could warrant your attention is toward the lake's southwest corner, where marshes and beaver ponds present some challenging fishing. If you do wander in that direction, you might also want to check out the Fall River inlet at Fan Lake's west end. The river parallels Old Fall River Road for several miles and has some enjoyable fishing, mainly for brookies and an occasional cutt, brown, or rainbow.

Lily Lake

Access: West of Route 7, opposite Lily Lake Visitor Center (Area 3); elevation 8,400 feet
Miles: Roadside
Species: Greenback cutt
Regulations: Catch-and-release, barbless single hook, artificial only

Float tube heaven. Once you're out in the middle of Lily Lake or near the lake's west end, take a look east. Those amazing mountains are The Crags. Lily Lake's gorgeous views and easy access have prompted television and movie location shoots there. Though there's no handicapped access per se, the lake is close to a parking area and once you're in or near the water, there's little to interfere with casting. A couple of my friends who must use wheelchairs find Lily Lake a good place to fish, possibly the best in the Park.

Until their acquisition by the Park Service a few years ago, the lake and surrounding land were privately owned and off limits to the public. When the lake opened to fishing, I'd already heard stories of the many good-sized greenbacks there. On my first trip I stayed intent on presenting various midge patterns and damselfly nymphs, with great results. I had been standing in waist-high water at the lake's west end for about thirty minutes. Once I moved back onto shore, I saw that my neoprene waders, from waist-level down to the boots, were strangely discolored and—moving! The neoprenes were covered with what must have been thousands of scuds (freshwater shrimp), tan and grayish white, about size #18. The presence of so many scuds explains the cutts' rapid growth rates and their propensity for cruising the shorelines. In fact, Lily Lake scuds make such easy and numerous targets for the trout that artificial scud patterns just don't produce that well there.

Damselfly nymphs rate among the favorite trout foods in Lily Lake. Damsel patterns tied with eyes seem to work better than those tied without them. Besides the Olive Damsel Nymph (#12 to #16), Hill's Stillborn Midge (#20 to #24) is another trout-catcher. Other effective patterns include: Olive Hare's Ear, #10 to #14; Griffith's Gnat, #18 to #22; and caddisflies, #12 to #16.

Colorado River

Access: West of Trail Ridge Road (Areas 12–14); elevations 8,500 to 9,200 feet
Miles: Roadside and trail
Hike: Easy to moderate
Species: Brook, rainbow, brown, cutt
Regulations: Rocky Mountain National Park
Camping: At confluence with Timber Creek
Horse trail: No

As I prepared for my first Colorado River fishing trip years ago in the Park, I envisioned an imposing water at least a hundred feet across. In fact, most of the Colorado is barely larger than the Big Thompson. Nevertheless, within the Park, the Colorado (properly termed The North Fork of the Colorado River) flows about fifteen miles, most of it paralleling Trail Ridge Road.

Area 12

If you enjoy fly fishing for brookies, try the river along the La Poudre Pass Trail, which heads north toward Lulu City, an old mining town site. Along this route, the Colorado has lots of brush, fast water, and plenty of aggressive brook trout. The Western Coachman and Elkhair Caddis (sizes #12 to #16) number among the best dry flies. Gold-Ribbed Hare's Ears and Bird's Stonefly nymphs (sizes #10 to #14) are safe bets subsurface. Big Dutch Creek enters the Colorado from the west side about 1.5 miles up the trail. It has some hard-to-catch cutts and cuttbows as well as many less discerning brookies.

Area 13

To the south of the La Poudre Pass Trail and just to the west of Trail Ridge Road, the river feeds out into a half-mile cluster of beaver ponds. Nearly all look wonderful, and some are, but not all hold trout. Don't get stubborn. If one pond fails to produce, move on to the next. Easy to say, hard to do. Yet that's the case with all ponds along the river, including the ones you'll come across in the Kawuneeche Valley.

Area 14

The river begins to flow through the valley at the Never Summer Ranch, moving south until outside Park boundaries. It's difficult to approach fishing the Colorado in the Kawuneeche Valley with a clear head and well-defined strategy. Wander a few hundred yards west of the river and you're spellbound by ponds and wetlands beckoning you away from the big water. At the same time, you know the Colorado's riffles and runs hold wonderful browns and rainbows. Fishing here takes time and thought. Even a small area of beaver ponds and little creeks merits many hours of exploration, observation, and fishing. The same goes for the river. Decide in advance where you're going to fish, and stick with your plan. Otherwise, you'll likely end up stymied and tired by the vastness, beauty, and angling potential of the locale. Most of your Colorado River fishing will be short-line, with emphasis on caddis, mayfly, and stonefly patterns, usually in that order of importance. Compared to East Slope waters, caddisflies tend to run a bit larger on the Colorado, so stock up on #12 and #14 Elkhair Caddis dry flies in tan or gray. The beaver waters require use of techniques and patterns discussed in Chapter 2.

Onahu Creek

Access: Onahu Creek Trailhead (Area 15); elevation 8,800 feet
Miles: 2.5
Hike: Moderate
Elevation: 9,300 feet
Species: Brook, rainbow
Regulations: Rocky Mountain National Park
Camping: Yes
Horse trail: Yes

For about a mile north of the trailhead, brookie-filled Onahu Creek moves through gently sloping terrain. Most of this stretch of the creek parallels the Onahu Creek Trail which, after about three miles, intersects the Long Meadows Trail. Upstream of that point the water steepens, and wild rainbows appear with more frequency. (If you head south on the Onahu Creek Trail for about two miles, you'll arrive at the Big Meadows section of Tonahutu Creek, described later.)

As you fish and hike in the Onahu area, pay close attention to where you are in relation to the trail and the creek itself. Several good tributaries flow into the Onahu, so it's easy to lose track of your position. In fact, the first substantial water crossed by the trail is not the Onahu, but a feeder creek. As a rule, it's not worth fishing more than about a mile above the Onahu Bridge. However, the first feeder creek about .25-mile to the north and west of the bridge runs through the pretty little valley of Long Meadows—still more good brookie fishing there.

Alternately, you can reach the creek south of the trailhead and west of Trail Ridge Road, where it's often mistaken for the Colorado River (which is farther west). The Onahu flows into the southern end of the Kawuneeche Valley, with lovely meadow fishing mainly for brookies and a few browns.

Timber Lake

Access: Timber Lake Trailhead (Area 11); elevation 9,000 feet
Miles: 5
Hike: Moderate to difficult
Destination elevation: 10,100 feet
Species: Greenback cutt
Regulations: Rocky Mountain National Park
Camping: Yes
Horse trail: Yes

The five-mile trip includes an elevation gain that exceeds two thousand feet—that's tough even by Park standards. Once you cross the Beaver Creek bridge you begin a seemingly endless ascent as the trail winds south, then east, through the woods. You won't see water again for about 2.5 miles, when the trail finally begins to parallel Timber Creek. Keep an eye out for wildflowers—some of the best you'll see in the Park. At that point you're just about halfway to the lake. The first time I arrived at Timber Lake, I felt a little disappointed (and spoiled). Compared with places like Fern Lake and The Loch, Timber seemed almost stark—no panoramic views or towering peaks here. My attitude changed once I began fishing. The ten-acre water is great fun, especially along its northern shoreline near the outlet creek. Try #18 Hare's Ears and Beadhead Soft-Hackles subsurface. Small mayflies and caddisflies (#16 to #18) are good dry-fly choices, as are ants and midges, #16 to #20.

Tonahutu Creek, Haynach Lakes

Access: Green Mountain Trailhead (Area 16); elevation 8,800 feet
Miles: 2
Hike: Moderate
Destination elevation: 9,300 feet
Species: Brook, rainbow
Regulations: Rocky Mountain National Park
Camping: Yes
Horse trail: Yes

A two-mile hike along the Green Mountain Trail brings you to the Tonahutu in Big Meadows and some especially fine meadow fishing for brook trout. About a mile upstream of Big Meadows the creek becomes more steep and fast-flowing. As with the Onahu, pay attention to the feeder creeks. Though some may fish well, they can throw you way off track. Tonahutu's first conspicuous feeder enters from the north about 1.5 miles from your entrance into Big Meadows. The next one occurs on the creek's south side, around Granite Falls. Near the falls, get ready for wild rainbows and some cutts. Above Granite Falls, the creek flows about a mile through Tonahutu Meadows, with even more good fishing for rainbows, cutts, and brookies.

Once you're through the meadows, you'll see another feeder creek on the north side, and to its east a foot trail (no horses allowed). If you feel ambitious and strong, follow the foot trail up about 1.5 miles to the little 11,100-foot-high Haynach Lakes and their hybrid cutts.

Big Crystal Lake

Access: Lawn Lake Trailhead (Area 1); elevation 8,500 feet
Miles: 8
Hike: Very difficult
Destination elevation: 11,500 feet
Species: Greenback cutt
Regulations: Catch-and-release, barbless single hook, artificial only
Camping: No
Horse trail: No

En route to Big Crystal, the end of the line for horseback riding and camping is at Lawn Lake, roughly two miles east and south. About a half-mile east of Big Crystal Lake you'll pass barren Little Crystal Lake. It's fooled and disappointed quite a few overtired, overanxious anglers.

Big Crystal lives up to its name—almost twenty-five acres of clear water that reaches depths of over one hundred feet. It holds only greenbacks, many of them good-sized. The lake is a magnificent place, with Mummy Mountain, Hague's Peak, Fairchild Mountain, and Ypsilon Mountain—all near or over 13,500 feet—to the east, north, west, and southwest, respectively. Small (#16) Bead-head Soft-Hackles in tans or grays are effective patterns, as are #16 to #20 Brassies, Hill's Stillborn Midges, and Griffith's Gnats. The outlet at the lake's west end is Roaring River, which feeds into Lawn Lake.

Lawn Lake

Access: Lawn Lake Trailhead (Area 1); elevation 8,500 feet
Miles: 6
Hike: Difficult
Destination elevation: 11,000 feet
Species: Greenback cutt
Regulations: Catch-and-release, barbless single hook, artificial only

Camping: Yes
Horse trail: Yes

Twenty acres in size and twenty feet deep, Lawn Lake was even larger and deeper before its dam gave out in the 1982 flood that bears its name. All of Lawn Lake fishes well, though the Roaring River inlet and outlet areas are particularly enjoyable. Watch for cruising and sunning greenbacks along the entire shoreline. Dry-fly fishing with a small (#16 to #18) caddis or Parachute Adams can be especially good in these areas. During midsummer afternoons pay special attention to the lake's northeastern shores; try #18 black ants on the surface, and #16 Pheasant Tails below.

Cony Creek

Access: Wild Basin Trailhead (Area 6); elevation 8,500 feet
Miles: 2
Hike: Easy to moderate
Destination elevation: 9,500 feet
Species: Greenback cutt
Regulations: Catch-and-release, barbless single hook, artificial only
Camping: No
Horse trail: No

After two miles on the trail, watch for Calypso Cascades. Cony Creek is the stream on the west side. Here you leave the trail behind, so get ready, if you like, for some pretty heavy-duty brush-filled hiking and wading. The terrain and water do flatten out some about 1.5 miles above the cascades—with more fine fishing but still not easy going. The nearest trail along there is the Finch Lake Trail, which, from the west end of Finch Lake, roughly parallels Cony Creek on its north side.

Small, fast, rocky, and brushy, Cony has dense hatches of mayflies, midges, caddis, and stoneflies—all appreciated by greenbacks and maniacal fly anglers. Conditions require quick short-line presentations.

Cony Creek is fed by Hutcheson Lakes, some of the best—and least fished—greenback waters in the Park.

Hutcheson Lakes

Access: Finch Lake Trailhead (Area 5); elevation 8,500 feet
Miles: 9
Hike: Very difficult
Destination elevation: 10,900 feet
Species: Greenback cutt
Regulations: Catch-and-release, barbless single hook, artificial only
Camping: No
Horse trail: No

This is no day trip. Pear Lake, about a half-mile to the northeast of Lower Hutcheson and just a few hundred feet lower, has both horseback access and camping; it's your best choice for a home base. Because of their remote location and prime habitat, the Hutcheson Lakes have terrific fishing for greenbacks.

If you head due south from Pear Lake, you'll connect with the upper reaches of Cony Creek. Follow Cony upstream to the first lake, Lower Hutcheson. Don't be fooled by the Lower Hutcheson's small size (just a couple of acres)—it's a dandy. Follow its inlet a few hundred yards upstream to the even smaller Middle Hutcheson Lake, another superb fishery. From there, it's a little less than a mile to the highest, and I think the best, water of the three: Upper Hutcheson Lake. On your way, don't overlook some lovely ponded sections of the creek. Above Upper Hutcheson, Cony Lake also holds cutts and has, in my experience, some of the most unpredictable fishing in the Park. Although I wouldn't recommend Cony as a destination in itself, if you've gone as far as Upper Hutcheson, hike in the extra quarter-mile and check out Cony Lake.

Pear Lake

Access: Finch Lake Trailhead (Area 5); elevation 8,500 feet
Miles: 7
Hike: Very difficult
Destination elevation: 10,600 feet
Species: Greenback cutt
Regulations: Catch-and-release, barbless single hook, artificial only
Camping: Yes
Horse trail: Yes

On some older maps you'll see this seventeen-acre water labeled a reservoir, not a lake. Reservoir operations ceased several years ago, though you can still see remnants of the old dam. Thanks to the surrounding terrain, Pear Lake can absorb a fair bit of sunlight and warmth on summer days, stimulating the surface activities of insects and cutts.

To the northwest and southwest, Mount Copeland and Elk Tooth, respectively, are both about 13,000 feet high. As the sun dips behind them, expect air temperatures to drop—quickly. Even so, the evening rises here can last an inordinately long time. If you're lucky, you may find yourself casting dry flies or emergers in the alpenglow, a pinkish light that reflects off mountain peaks long after sunset.

Ouzel Creek

Access: Wild Basin Trailhead (Area 6); elevation 8,500 feet
Miles: 2.5
Hike: Moderate
Destination elevation: 9,400 feet
Species: Greenback cutt
Regulations: Catch-and-release, barbless single hook, artificial only
Camping: No
Horse trail: No

Here's another trip through brush and bugs, as trying and potentially satisfying as the one described for Cony Creek. Note that above Ouzel Falls, Ouzel Creek is roughly paralleled by the Bluebird Lake Trail, which leads to Ouzel Lake.

Ouzel Lake

Access: Wild Basin Trailhead (Area 6); elevation 8,500 feet
Miles: 5
Hike: Moderate to slightly difficult
Destination elevation: 10,000 feet
Species: Greenback cutt
Regulations: Catch-and-release, barbless single hook, artificial only
Camping: Yes
Horse trail: Yes

A six-acre gem of a lake, loaded with cutts. About 1.5 miles up from the trailhead, turn west onto the clearly marked Bluebird Lake Trail; avoid the foot trail located about a quarter-mile to the east and north. Once on the Bluebird Lake Trail, make sure you watch for the fork that heads south to your destination. Otherwise you might end up fishing tiny Chickadee Pond—less than an acre in size, just a few feet deep, and barren. It lies a few hundred yards to the northeast of Ouzel Lake. Ouzel Creek enters at Ouzel Lake's southern corner and flows out its eastern side.

Sandbeach Lake and Sandbeach Creek

Access: Sandbeach Lake Trailhead at Copeland Lake (Area 4); elevation 8,300 feet
Miles: 4.5
Hike: Very difficult
Destination elevation: 10,300 feet
Species: Greenback cutt

Regulations: Catch-and-release, barbless single hook, artificial only
Camping: Yes
Horse trail: Yes

The route to Sandbeach Lake always gives me a renewed respect and love for good trail horses. Hiking and climbing two thousand feet in 4.5 miles just isn't fun—even if the destination is one of
my favorites for greenback fishing.

Sandbeach Lake covers about seventeen acres; its greatest depth
measures around forty feet. Though all the lake has superb fishing,
I've always been partial to its southern end, where the lake flows
down into Sandbeach Creek. Check out the creek from the lake to
at least a mile downstream—the tiny riffles, rapids, and glides all
hold cutts.

Grand Lake

Access: East of Trail Ridge Road (Area 16); elevation 8,400 feet
Miles: Roadside
Species: Brown, laker, kokanee, rainbow
Regulations: State of Colorado and as posted

Prepare to set aside many of the fly-fishing concepts and
equipment guidelines discussed so far and consider some new ones.
Almost three hundred feet deep in some places, the five-hundred-
acre Grand Lake is Colorado's largest natural lake. Though just outside Park boundaries, the lake is mentioned here both because of
its beauty and its good-sized fish. Two neighboring lakes, Lake
Granby and Shadow Mountain Reservoir, are prone to greatly fluc-
tuating water levels due to dam controls, but Grand Lake is not. Major fish species are rainbow, kokanee salmon, brown trout, and lake
trout (lakers or mackinaw). Lakers weighing more than twenty
pounds are not uncommon. Since Grand Lake's salmon and lakers
present the greatest fly-angling challenges, the tackle and techniques discussed here center on those two species.

Winds, storms, and waves can make Grand Lake extremely dangerous, so float tubing is not advised. Fishing from shore or wade-fishing is limited by private ownership of much of the lake's shoreline, so boat fishing is the way to go. A sturdy motorboat (rentals are available through local marinas) will give you the ability to cover water as well as the means to reach shelter in foul weather. A warning: Never, ever try to ride out a storm on Grand Lake. The waters can be extremely treacherous and have claimed many lives.

Rigging Up

The best times to fish Grand Lake are from spring ice-out through the end of June. During that period, salmon and lake trout leave deeper water and begin to cruise and feed at depths ranging from ten to fifty feet. Later in the season, as water temperatures rise, the bigger fish return to greater depths and become more difficult to catch. The lake then also gets used more for nonfishing recreational activities. You'll occasionally see rising trout, usually rainbows, so you may want to bring along a comparatively light rig (a nine-foot 6/7-weight is ideal) to fish on or near the surface. Generally though, a heavier outfit is what you'll use the most. Just to give you an idea of the size and appetite of Grand Lake's big trout and salmon, the favorite bait of experienced ice fishermen there is a whole dead sucker at least eight inches long.

I use a nine-foot, 9-weight rod set up with a weight-forward 10-weight line and a disc-drag reel. Taking a twenty-pound fish on lighter tackle is exhausting both to you and your quarry. The heavy-duty rod and reel are equal to the task, giving the extra power you'll need for casting and lifting. (The rig can also be used for pike, large bass, and for general saltwater fishing.) Don't bother with a floating line. I generally use either a Class V full-sinking line or a Class III sinking-tip line (sink rates of about six inches and four inches per second, respectively). Both lines are much harder to lift from the water than a floating line, but once a sinking line is airborne, it casts pretty easily. Leaders should be seven to eight feet long and tapered down to 3X or heavier.

Bring a long-handled landing net, too. You can make one from a cheap oversized over-the-shoulder model and a few spare parts. Remove the grip, jam a length of aluminum tubing onto the handle, and secure the tubing with hose clamps—inelegant, but practical.

One of the biggest problems of fly fishing from a boat is that of fouled line—line that gets caught underfoot, tangled around a gas can, or wrapped on an oar or your ankle. The fouled line will not only interfere with casting and retrieving; in the worst case, it will prevent you from playing or even catching a fish. So, you should always use a stripping basket to hold excess line. You can purchase a basket or make one by drilling one-inch-diameter drainage holes in the bottom of a rectangular plastic washbasin.

Deep Water, Big Fish, Old Tricks

Fishing deep water requires that you keep track of line depth. Once the line is out on the water, count aloud ("one-one hundred, two-one hundred," and so on) to help you measure and remember how far down the line is. For example, after making several unsuccessful presentations to a depth of thirty feet, it's possible that simply raising or lowering the presentation (and therefore, decreasing or increasing your count) may result in a fish.

The take of a large (over five pounds) trout or salmon can differ from that of a smaller fish. It's often felt as a series of three or four taps or tugs at the end of the line *before* the ultimate solid take. Set the hook too early, lose a fish. It takes a certain discipline for the angler to await, judge, and act upon the "real" take, but patience and experience will pay off. Seldom should you set the hook on the first sign of a take unless it's rippingly strong, in which case the fish often hooks itself anyway. If you do get an apparently solid hookup but then miss it, never pick up and recast. The same fish (or another) may still be interested.

Once a fish is on, always assume it's a big one, especially since it often will be. Depending on the fish's species, strength, and size, the landing process may take from a few minutes to the better part of half an hour. As always, good line control is essential: play the fish from the reel. The reel's drag setting should be set for moderate resistance. Once hooked, lake trout and kokanee salmon seldom jump from the water. However, they can and often do swim marvelously fast, alternately stopping and holding and diving deep. If you have a fair bit of line out, say seventy feet or more, there's a chance that you'll go into your backing, so be sure that the line-to-backing connection is solid and the backing itself is in good shape and of proper breaking test (twenty to thirty pounds).

When a hooked fish holds its position and refuses to move, it's said to sulk, and a sulking laker or kokanee poses some interesting problems to the fly angler. Your worst course of action is to pull as hard as you can against the fish in an attempt to move it because you risk breaking or considerably weakening your line-leader-fly connections. Your two best options are: (1) keeping a tight line and playing a waiting game, or (2) forcing the fish to move. Either one can work, but in case a fish is especially stubborn, I usually bring several baseball-sized rocks with me. I'll toss a few in the sulking fish's area to get the fish moving again. The technique sounds crude; maybe so, but it works. It's used frequently by British Isle and New England salmon anglers.

Another salmon-angling tradition that carries over into fishing big lakes for big fish is the use of streamers. I've found that hook sizes #1/0 to #6, all 2X or 3X long, work best, with a #4 being best all-round. I tie the streamers weighted and, once I'm ready to begin fishing, usually pinch one or two BB shots on the tippet about eight inches above the hook eye to help keep the fly down and counteract the leader's buoyancy. Favorite patterns are the Gray Ghost, Dahlberg Diver (black or olive), and Woolly Bugger (black or olive). Woolly Buggers tied with ice chenille work as well as or better than those tied with peacock herl. The cheeks on a Gray Ghost should strongly resemble fish eyes or gills; imitation jungle cock (black spotted with white and orange) works best. Dahlberg Divers should include moving doll eyes, about five millimeters in diameter.

Boat Fishing

When fishing from a boat, especially one that's not anchored, it's imperative that you get a fix on your position once you're out on the water. Otherwise you'll just drift aimlessly, and therefore fish ineffectively. Pick two conspicuous stationary objects as points of reference (for example, a boulder on the south shore and a tall tree on the north shore). Periodically check that you're staying within those general bounds, since winds and currents will, of course, move the boat. Repeat this procedure for every area you fish.

As you fish from a boat that's in a relatively fixed position, make each presentation in a calculated, methodical way. First, imagine that the boat's stern or bow is at twelve o'clock and work your presentations at every hour around an imaginary clock face until you return to your starting point. Second, vary the depth of each presentation, again working around the clock face.

As noted in Chapter 2, most streamer retrieves work best when performed at extremely slow or fast rates, though a quick twitch or pause may induce the strike you've been waiting for. If you do find that magical retrieve, it might well work for the rest of the day—or just for one fish. How a retrieved streamer "behaves" is usually more important than where it was initially placed. As you retrieve a streamer, think about how it might act if it were indeed alive. Is the streamer a fish that's dawdling, feeding, carefree, injured, or panic-stricken? Perhaps it's a caddis pupa drifting up to the surface. Experiment and use your imagination, together with rod and line, to give a streamer life and personality. To help the line stay submerged during a retrieve, point the rod tip down toward the water's surface. Conversely, to make the line ascend, keep the rod tip up.

Finding Fish

Many of the observations made in Chapter 2 on locating fish apply to Grand Lake. But Grand Lake's big trout and salmon are seldom seen or caught right next to the shoreline, as they prefer deeper waters generally not accessible to a shorebound angler. The problem gets to be that, unless you have some sophisticated navigational gear and the expertise to use it, you won't know for certain exactly where you are in relation to the bottom of the lake. While fly fishing large New England lakes and reservoirs, as well as the Atlantic Ocean off Cape Cod and Long Island, I usually bring a jury-rigged sounding line with me, and I continue to do this on Grand Lake trips. It's a one-hundred-yard spool of Dacron line with a heavy teardrop sinker tied to the end. The line is marked at ten- and twenty-foot intervals so I can read the water depth after the sinker hits bottom. By taking several soundings in the same general area, I can judge changes in the water depth. For example, if I'm above a lake bottom shelf, I might measure water depth of forty feet on one side of the boat and ninety feet on the other side.

You can use your eyes, too; shallow water appears much lighter in color than deep water. These transitional areas are some of the best to fish. With the right conditions and approach, you might see a full one hundred feet into the depths. Apart from a heavy surface chop or roily water, the biggest obstacle to your water vision is glare. The more glare you can block from your view and the closer you can get to the water's surface, the better you'll see into the lake. A hat and polarized sunglasses will help block out glare, as will cupping your hands around the sides of the sunglasses. Holding an opened umbrella over the water you want to view is another helpful technique, though you'll surely elicit some interesting comments from any onlookers. While in a boat, getting your face down close to the water is tricky and potentially hazardous, since you'll need to lean over the side. Don't even try it unless you have someone else on board to counteract your shifted weight and the water is relatively calm. Electronic fish finders can display water depth, fish location, and enemy submarines. It's your call, but I don't think sonar is sporting. Save your money for a cane rod.

The Release

Once you've found, fooled, played, and netted your monster catch, it's time to revive it. Hold the fish right side up in the water, one hand supporting it near its head, the other hand gripping just above the tail. Move the trout gently back and forth as it reacclimates and reoxygenates. Be gentle but firm: a large, powerful fish often seems ready to leave at the first opportunity, only to die soon afterward. As a rule, you should wait until the fish has made two or three *strong* efforts to escape—then set it free. And that's the grand sport on Grand Lake.

Closed Waters

At this writing, none of these areas is open to fishing at any time: Bear Lake and its inlet and outlet streams; Hunters Creek above Wild Basin Ranger Station; West Creek above the falls; above War Dance Falls, Bench Lake, and Ptarmigan Creek; Lake Nanita outlet for one hundred yards downstream of the lake. Hidden Valley Creek and Ponds are open to fishing only from August 1 to March 31 and are closed the rest of the year.

Barren Lakes

Here's a list of the Park's barren lakes: Andrews, Azure, Bierstadt, Bighorn, Blue, Bluebird, Castle, Chiquita, Cony, Chickadee, Chickaree, Chipmunk, Cub, Dunraven, Eagle, Embryo, Emerald, Falcon, Fifth, Finch, Frigid, Frozen, Green, Helene, Highest, Hourglass, Irene (both), Julian, Junco, Keplinger, Lark, Lion (both), Little Crystal, Lonesome, Louise, Love, Many Winds, Marigold (both), Murphy, Nokoni, Nymph, Pipit, Powell, Ptarmigan, Rainbow, Rowe, Shelf, Snowbank, Snowdrift, Spectacle (both), Sprague Glacier, Tourmaline, Two Rivers, and Upper Twin.

Appendix: A Beginner's Reference

Fly Casting Basics

These are guidelines and checkpoints for the analysis, under-standing, and improvement of basic casting skills. Books, video-tapes, and other tools (listed later) are available for anyone learning to cast, but there is absolutely no substitute for personalized in-struction. To best acquire any new skill, be it golf, piano playing, or fly casting, you need patience, practice, concentration, dedication, discipline, relaxation—and a good teacher!

What a Fly Rod Does

Fly casting differs markedly from spin or bait casting, where the weight of a lure or bait helps pull the line through the air. Instead, a fly rod is designed to throw the weight of its line, which in turn pro-pels the leader and fly. The rod works as an efficient, flexible lever that can store and release energy. To take advantage of rod design, use your casting arm and a moving fly line to bend the rod tip.

Where and How to Practice

An ideal practice area is on the water, but a lawn can also serve well. (A fly line will be worn by repeated contact with the ground, so keep a separate line for this use.) In place of a fly, attach a bit of brightly colored yarn to the leader.

1. Practice consistently; for example, every other day for thirty min-utes at a time.
2. Practice well. Constantly practicing bad habits can do more harm than no practice at all. Work with a qualified instructor to stay on track.
3. Forget about casting for distance. Learn to cast confidently with

no more than about twenty feet of line, always working toward a smooth, controlled, and delicate technique.

4. Practice accuracy on progressively smaller targets. Start with an inner tube or tire and work your way down to a briefcase, pie plate, then coffee mug.

5. Always watch what the rod and line are doing as you cast!

Preparation

Hands

Wherever practical, references to the right or left hand are omitted. Instead, the terms *rod hand* (the dominant hand that holds the rod) and *line hand* (the nondominant hand that controls the fly line) are used.

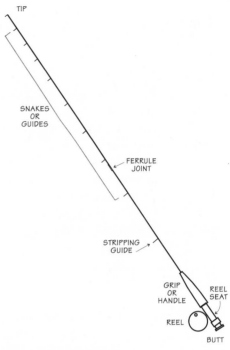

Fig. 12. Fly Rod Parts

Stance

To gain a comfortable and solid stance, position your left foot about twelve to sixteen inches in front of and roughly perpendicular to your right foot. If you are left-handed, reverse these directions. You should also be able to watch the rod and line as they move in back of and in front of you.

Line Length and Positioning

Practice casting with no more than about twenty feet of line coming off the rod tip. Straighten the line in front of you before beginning to cast.

Line Control

When casting, never allow slack line between the stripping guide and the reel. Any extra line should be spooled onto the reel or controlled by your line hand.

Grip

Hold the cork handle of the rod with a "handshake," placing your thumb on the upper part of the cork. Always keep your thumb pointed up toward the rod tip (see figure 13). The main force of your grip should come from your thumb and index finger; the other fingers help stabilize the rod.

Wrist and Elbow

Think of the rod as an extension of your forearm; do not flex your wrist while casting. All movement should come from your elbow. Avoid moving or rotating your shoulder or upper body. Hold the elbow of your casting arm about six inches away from the side of your body. Elbow position should remain constant throughout the casting motion. Never move your elbow forward and backward or side to side.

Casting Motion

The basic motion of casting is similar to that of picking up and then hanging up the handset of a wall-mounted telephone. Pick up the handset and bring it to your ear. That's the back cast. With the same degree of force used to pick it up, hang the handset back onto the wall. That's the forward cast.

A clock face is another helpful reference. On pick-up (back cast), the rod points back to about one o'clock. On hang-up (forward cast), the rod points forward to about eleven o'clock.

A Foundation

In large part, the quality of your back cast determines how good or bad the rest of your cast will be. For this reason, many people consider the back cast the foundation of casting. Five key elements need to be understood and practiced. The back cast should be:

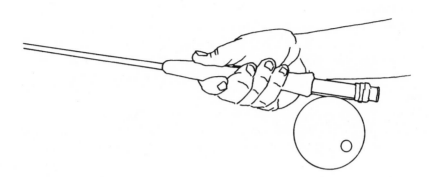

Fig. 13. A Proper Grip

1. STRONG. Move the rod back with a fair degree of strength. Most beginners tend to be overcautious, not putting enough momentum into the rod to drive out the line effectively.
2. SMOOTH. Do not jerk the rod back. Apply power smoothly and progressively.
3. SMALL. The rod tip should not go past the one o'clock position, especially when casting just twenty feet of line.
4. STOPPED. Stop the rod shaft when it appears to be about even with your shoulder.
5. SEEN! Watch rod and line movement during all phases of casting. There is no magic casting "feel" for most beginners.

The First Casts

Back Cast
1. Keep about twenty feet of line straightened in front of you. Angle the rod slightly away from your body. Point the rod tip down to and almost touch the water.
2. Bring the rod back on a vertical plane to a one o'clock position, gradually increasing rod speed as the fly line leaves the water. The line should travel up and in back of you. *Between the eleven o'clock and one o'clock positions, the rod tip must always move in a straight line!* Otherwise, a loop may not form.

3. Watch the line as it unrolls in the air in back of you. Observe the shape of the loop formed by the fly line. The loop should be fairly small and narrow if you stop the rod where indicated (see figure 14). (A larger, wider loop results from stopping the rod farther in back of you.)

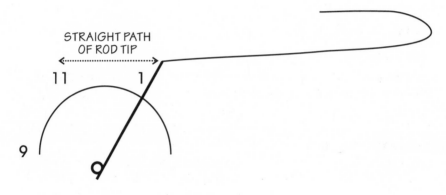

Fig. 14. Path of Rod Tip with Back-Cast Loop

4. Repeat steps 1 through 3 until you can consistently form small narrow loops with your back cast.

Pick-Up and Lay-Down Cast

Here the back cast will be followed by a forward cast and delivery of the line.

1. After making a back cast, watch the line as it forms a narrow loop in back of you. As the line is almost but not completely unrolled (figure 15) . . .

2. Bring the rod forward (as if hanging up the phone) to an eleven o'clock position, using the same degree of force as was applied to your back cast.

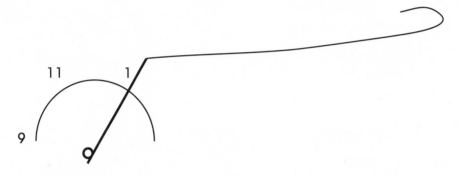

Fig. 15. Line Extension on the Back Cast

3. Watch the loop formed by the line during the forward cast. It should be as small and narrow as the one formed by your back cast (see figure 16).

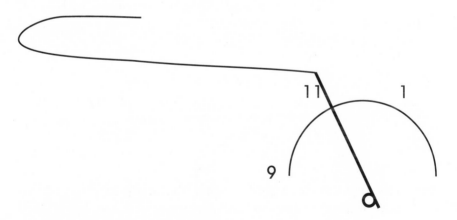

Fig. 16. Loop on the Forward Cast

4. Deliver the line. When the line is almost but not completely un-rolled, lower the rod to about a nine o'clock position, applying the same degree of force used during the back cast and the forward cast (see figure 17). The line should straighten in front of you.

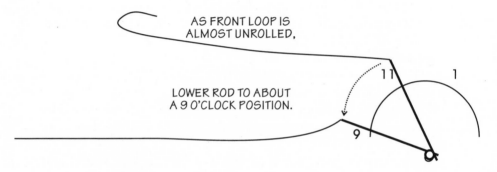

AS FRONT LOOP IS ALMOST UNROLLED,

LOWER ROD TO ABOUT A 9 O'CLOCK POSITION.

Fig. 17. Line Delivery

5. Repeat steps 1 through 4 until you can consistently form small narrow loops with both your back cast and forward cast and the line lies down fairly straight in front of you.

Pick-Up and Lay-Down Cast Notes
1. A popping, whip-cracking sound indicates that you have brought the line forward too quickly.
2. A collapsed, piled-up line results from waiting too long before beginning the forward cast.

Pick-Up and Lay-Down Cast with Shooting Line
From the reel, strip off about ten feet of line, forming a slack loop of reserve shooting line between the reel and stripping guide.

Position your line hand a few inches above and away from the rod handle. Hold on to the line at that point with the thumb, index, and middle fingers of your line hand. (The slack loop of reserve shooting line is now located between the reel and your line hand.) Your line hand should move with and remain close to the rod during all phases of the cast.

1. Make a back cast.
2. At the eleven o'clock position on your forward cast, let the loop of shooting line pass through the fingers of your line hand and through the rod guides.
3. Keep your line-hand fingers in light contact with the shooting line as it moves forward. (As you practice, vary the amount of shooting line that you release.)
4. Complete this cast as you did the pick-up and lay-down cast, lowering the rod to about a nine o'clock position. The line should straighten in front of you.
5. Strip back the line shot out during the cast and reform a ten-foot slack loop of shooting line between the reel and the fingers of your line hand.
6. Repeat steps 1 through 5 until you can consistently control and release the shooting line.

False-Casting
This method of casting keeps the line airborne to dry out a soaked fly or to measure out required distance. It's often used as a way to begin a cast.

1. Make a back cast.
2. Make a forward cast.
3. Repeat steps 1 and 2 twice more.
4. Complete the cast as you did the pick-up and lay-down cast, lowering the rod to about a nine o'clock position. The line should straighten in front of you.

False-Casting Notes
When an angler learns to false-cast, the most common errors include:

1. Moving the rod and line too quickly and not allowing sufficient time for the line to extend on the back cast and forward cast.
2. Allowing the forward cast to dip down past the eleven o'clock position.
3. Applying insufficient force to either the back cast, forward cast, or both.

An effective false cast is symmetrical:

1. Both back cast and forward cast should move through the same range and space of motion.
2. Both back cast and forward cast should form nearly identical loops.
3. Equal force should be applied to the back cast and the forward cast.
4. During the back cast and forward cast, the rod tip must always move in a straight line and remain in the same horizontal plane between the eleven o'clock and one o'clock positions.

These instructions call for a maximum of three false casts before executing the final forward cast and delivery of the fly line. The reason behind this is that the more time your line spends in the air instead of in the water, the less likely you are to catch fish—and the more likely you are to foul your cast.

Once you've learned how to false-cast, learn to add and control shooting line.

Slack-Line Cast

A slack-line cast makes the line lie out in curves on the water and helps delay drag.

1. Stop your final forward cast at the eleven o'clock position.
2. Immediately lower the rod to about a nine o'clock position (see figure 18).

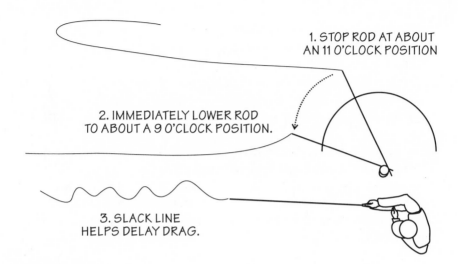

1. STOP ROD AT ABOUT
AN 11 O'CLOCK POSITION

2. IMMEDIATELY LOWER ROD
TO ABOUT A 9 O'CLOCK POSITION.

3. SLACK LINE
HELPS DELAY DRAG.

Fig. 18. Slack-Line Cast

Presentations

Up-and-Across

This is a popular and effective method with which to present a dry fly or nymph. Remember to hold the line between the index and middle fingers of your rod hand as soon as you complete the cast.

1. Cast the fly upstream and slightly across-stream of the target area (see figure 19).
2. Hold the rod at about a ten o'clock position.
3. The current carries the fly to its downstream destination.

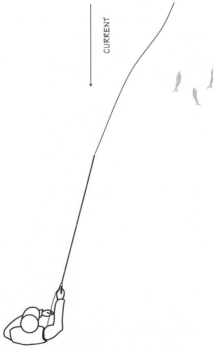

Fig. 19. Up-and-Across Presentation

Up-and-Across Presentation Notes

As the fly moves downstream,

1. Retrieve line in time with the drift of the fly.
2. Follow the drift with the rod tip and with your body.
3. Let the fly continue to drift until it begins to drag, then recast.

Down-and-Across Slack-Line

Chapter 2 describes a down-and-across presentation for a streamer. Coupled with a slack-line cast, the presentation works well for dry flies and nymphs. Again, remember to hold the line between the index and middle fingers of your rod hand as soon as you complete the cast.

1. Cast the fly downstream and slightly across-stream of the target area (see figure 20).

2. Hold the rod at about a ten o'clock position.

3. The current carries the fly to its downstream destination.

Down-and-Across Slack-Line Presentation Notes

As the fly moves downstream,

1. Follow the drift with the rod tip and with your body.
2. Let the fly continue to drift until it begins to drag, then recast.

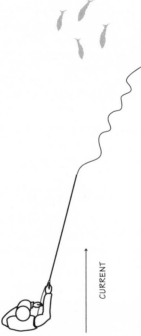

Fig. 20. Down-and-Across Slack-Line Presentation

You can also use slack-line casts for up-and-across presentations where drag and currents pose problems.

Equipment

Beginners in any sport seldom want to invest in top-of-the-line equipment, though it's easier to use and expedites learning. If you think you might be serious about fly fishing, start right and buy the best equipment you can afford. A specialty fly-fishing shop offers the greatest value in products and services. (Chapter 6 contains additional information on equipment.)

Leaders

A leader is tapered monofilament. At one end it's attached to the fly line, at the other end it's attached to the fly. Commonly used leaders vary in length from seven to fifteen feet. An approximately nine-foot leader fits most purposes.

Knotless leaders are manufactured from a single strand of monofilament; knotted leaders are made from lengths of mono that are tied together. Knotless leaders are well suited for slipping cleanly through algae- and weed-laden waters where a knotted leader might become fouled.

Tippet

Tippet is measured in X sizes. The most commonly used tippet sizes in the Park are 4X through 6X (diameters .007 to .005 of an inch). The breaking-pound-test of 4X, 5X, and 6X leaders now averages around 6, 4.5, and 3.5 pounds, respectively. 5X is your best all-round choice.

Hooks

Hook sizes are classed by number, with a #28 being one of the smallest (you can fit a dozen on a dime without one hook touching any other). As hook sizes increase, the numbers decrease. A #12 is larger than a #14, a #4 larger than a #8, and so on. A #14 or #16 will fit most of your needs.

Here's a rule to determine what size tippet is most appropriate to a hook: divide hook size by four and add one. For example, #16 hook divided by 4 = 4 + 1 = 5X.

Knots

Learn to tie a knot that's new to you by using quarter-inch rope, gradually working down to string, heavy monofilament, and tippet. To maximize the durability and strength of any fishing knot, you must perform these steps *before* drawing it tight:

1. Wet the knot with water or saliva.
2. Pull the knot closed *quickly* and *smoothly*.
3. Trim excess line close to the finished knot.

Here are some of the strongest and most useful fishing knots and their applications.

Fig. 21. Improved clinch knot. This knot is used to attach the fly to the tippet. *(Knot Drawings by Heidi Greenwood Pate)*

Fig. 22. Blood knot. This knot is used to join two lines of similar diameter.

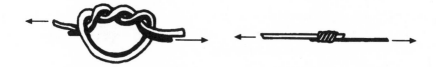

Fig. 23. Surgeon's knot. This knot may be used to join two lines of similar or different diameter.

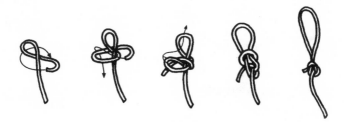

Fig. 24. Perfection loop. This knot joins leader to tippet.

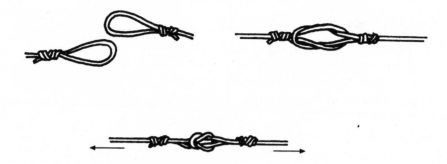

Fig. 25. Loop-to-loop connection. Use this connection to interlock two perfection loops.

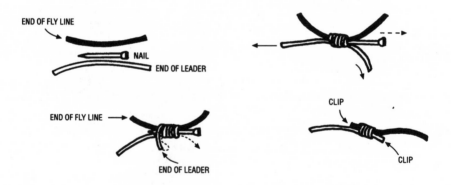

Fig. 26. Nail knot. Use the nail knot to join leader to fly line.

Since the nail knot requires using an obect like a nail or hollow tube, you might just as well buy a gadget like an Easy-Tie or Tie-Fast tool to make the job much quicker and easier.

Bibliography

Bates, Joseph. *Streamer Fly Tying and Fishing*. Harrisburg, Penn.: Stackpole Books, 1966.

Bergman, Ray. *Trout*. New York: Alfred A. Knopf, 1949.

Borger, Gary. *Nymphing*. Harrisburg, Penn.: Stackpole Books, 1979.

Engle, Ed. *Fly Fishing the Tailwaters*. Harrisburg, Penn.: Stackpole Books, 1991.

Harvey, George. *Techniques of Trout Fishing and Fly Tying*. New York: Lyons and Burford, 1990.

Hill, Roger. *Fly Fishing the South Platte River*. Boulder, Colo.: Pruett Publishing Company, 1991.

Jaworowski, Ed. *The Cast*. Harrisburg, Penn.: Stackpole Books, 1992.

Kreh, Lefty, and Mark Sosin. *Practical Fishing Knots*. New York: Nick Lyons Books, 1972.

Marinaro, Vince. *A Modern Dry-Fly Code*. New York: Putnam's Sons, 1950.

Swisher, Doug, and Carl Richards. *Selective Trout*. New York: Crown, 1971.

Trails Illustrated. *Topographical Map #200, Rocky Mountain National Park*. Evergreen, Colo.: Trails Illustrated. (Phone: 800-962-1643)

Wulff, Joan. *Joan Wulff's Fly-Casting Techniques*. New York: Nick Lyons Books, 1987. (Videotapes available.)

Index